Attitude Intelligence Vol I

Attitude, Volume 1

BANTAR-SHEY

Published by PHOENIX HEIGHTS INCORP, 2023.

ATTITUDE INTELLIGENCE VOL I

First edition. December 5, 2023.

ISBN: 979-8223758662

Written by BANTAR-SHEY.

Table of Contents

Attitude Intelligence Vol I 1
BOOK OVERVIEW 2
Introduction to Attitude Intelligence 5
Attitude Intelligence in Personal Relationships 20
Attitude Intelligence in Professional Life 31
Attitude Intelligence in Health and Well-Being 53
Attitude Intelligence in Personal Development 64
Attitude Intelligence in Financial Success 78
Attitude Intelligence in Education 93
Attitude Intelligence in Parenting 107
Attitude Intelligence in Interactions 120
Attitude Intelligence in Personal Happiness 135
Attitude Intelligence in Overcoming Challenges 149
Conclusion 163

This book is dedicated to my Grand Mother Mrs. Shey Magdalene Mafor, in memory of my Grand Father Mr. Shey Emmanuel Bantar. In addition, it is also dedicated to all the knowledge, understanding & wisdom seekers in the world. Thank you.

Preface

BOOK OVERVIEW

In "Attitude Intelligence," we explore the power of attitude and its impact on every aspect of life. This book delves into the concept of attitude intelligence, which goes beyond mere positivity or negativity. Attitude intelligence is about understanding and harnessing the power of our attitudes to shape our thoughts, emotions, and actions in a way that leads to personal growth and success. Through practical strategies and real-life examples, this book provides insights on how to develop and cultivate a positive attitude intelligence that can transform our relationships, careers, health, and overall well-being.

By examining the role of attitude intelligence in various areas of life, this book offers a comprehensive guide to understanding and improving our attitudes. From the workplace to personal relationships, from health and wellness to achieving goals, "Attitude Intelligence" provides practical tools and techniques to enhance our attitude intelligence in every aspect of life. With a focus on self-awareness, emotional intelligence, and mindset shifts, this book empowers readers to take control of their attitudes and create positive change. Whether you are seeking personal growth, professional success, or improved well-being, this book will help you unlock the power of attitude intelligence to transform your life.

Part One

Chapter 1

ATTITUDE INTELLIGENCE VOL I

Introduction to Attitude Intelligence

1.1 Understanding Attitude Intelligence

Attitude Intelligence is a concept that encompasses the understanding and application of attitude in every aspect of life. It is the ability to recognize the power of attitude and harness it to achieve personal growth, success, and happiness. Attitude Intelligence goes beyond simply having a positive mindset; it involves developing a deep understanding of how attitude influences our thoughts, emotions, behaviors, and interactions with others.

At its core, Attitude Intelligence is about self-awareness and self-management. It is the ability to recognize and control our attitudes, beliefs, and reactions in different situations. By cultivating Attitude Intelligence, we can navigate through life's challenges with resilience, adaptability, and a positive outlook.

Attitude Intelligence is not limited to a specific domain; it applies to every aspect of life. Whether it is personal relationships, professional life, health and well-being, personal development, financial success, education, parenting, social interactions, or personal happiness, Attitude Intelligence plays a crucial role in shaping our experiences and outcomes.

In personal relationships, Attitude Intelligence helps us understand the impact of our attitudes on our interactions with others. It enables us to communicate effectively, build healthy relationships, resolve conflicts, and maintain a positive attitude even in challenging situations. By developing Attitude Intelligence in our relationships, we can foster trust, empathy, and mutual understanding.

In the professional realm, Attitude Intelligence is essential for career success. It involves developing a winning attitude at work, embracing leadership qualities, managing stress, and maintaining a healthy work-life balance. Attitude Intelligence empowers individuals to overcome obstacles, adapt to changes, and continuously grow professionally.

Attitude Intelligence also plays a significant role in health and well-being. Research has shown that a positive attitude can improve physical health, boost mental well-being, and enhance emotional resilience. By cultivating a positive attitude, individuals can reduce stress, increase their overall happiness, and improve their overall quality of life.

In personal development, Attitude Intelligence is crucial for building self-confidence, setting and achieving goals, overcoming obstacles, and embracing a mindset of continuous learning. It helps individuals develop a growth mindset, which is essential for personal growth and success.

Attitude Intelligence extends to financial success as well. It involves developing a positive money mindset, building wealth, making sound financial decisions, and achieving financial independence. By adopting a positive attitude towards money and financial matters, individuals can attract abundance and create a secure financial future.

In education, Attitude Intelligence plays a vital role in learning, motivation, academic success, and developing a growth mindset. It helps individuals approach learning with enthusiasm, embrace challenges, and persevere through setbacks. Attitude Intelligence empowers students to unlock their full potential and achieve academic excellence.

Attitude Intelligence is also essential in parenting. It influences parent-child relationships, discipline strategies, teaching resilience, and nurturing a positive attitude in children. By modeling a positive attitude, parents can inspire their children to develop a positive outlook on life and navigate challenges with confidence.

In social interactions, Attitude Intelligence promotes empathy, building connections, cultural sensitivity, and promoting a positive attitude in society. It enables individuals to understand and appreciate diverse perspectives, foster inclusivity, and contribute to a harmonious and supportive community.

Lastly, Attitude Intelligence is closely linked to personal happiness. It involves cultivating a positive attitude, practicing gratitude, embracing mindfulness, and finding joy in everyday life. By developing Attitude Intelligence, individuals can experience greater happiness, fulfillment, and overall well-being.

In conclusion, Attitude Intelligence is a comprehensive concept that applies to every aspect of life. It is about understanding and harnessing the power of attitude to achieve personal growth, success, and happiness. By developing Attitude Intelligence, individuals can navigate through life's challenges with resilience, adaptability, and a positive outlook. It is a lifelong journey of self-awareness, self-management, and continuous growth.

1.2 The Importance of Attitude in Life

Attitude plays a crucial role in shaping our lives and influencing our experiences. It is the lens through which we perceive and interpret the world around us. Attitude intelligence, the ability to understand and manage our attitudes effectively, is essential for personal growth, success, and overall well-being. In this section, we will explore the importance of attitude in various aspects of life and how it impacts our relationships, career, health, personal development, finances, education, parenting, social interactions, happiness, and overcoming challenges.

Attitude and Relationships

Our attitude significantly affects our relationships with others. A positive attitude fosters healthy connections, enhances communication, and promotes understanding and empathy. It allows us to approach conflicts with a constructive mindset, seeking resolutions rather than escalating tensions. On the other hand, a negative attitude can strain relationships, create misunderstandings, and hinder effective communication. By cultivating a positive attitude, we can build and maintain strong, fulfilling relationships.

Attitude and Career Success

Attitude plays a vital role in our professional lives. Employers value individuals with a positive attitude as they tend to be more motivated, adaptable, and resilient. A positive attitude at work fosters a productive and harmonious environment, enhances teamwork, and promotes creativity and innovation. It also helps us navigate challenges and setbacks with a solution-oriented mindset, leading to personal and career growth.

Attitude and Health

Our attitude has a profound impact on our physical and mental well-being. Research has shown that a positive attitude can improve immune function, reduce stress levels, and enhance overall health. It enables us to cope better with adversity, recover from illnesses faster, and maintain a healthier lifestyle. Conversely, a negative attitude can contribute to stress-related disorders, weaken the immune system, and hinder our ability to bounce back from setbacks. By cultivating a positive attitude, we can promote better health and well-being.

Attitude and Personal Development

Attitude is a key factor in personal development and self-improvement. A positive attitude fuels self-confidence, resilience, and the belief in our abilities to overcome challenges and achieve our goals. It enables us to embrace continuous learning, seek opportunities for growth, and develop a growth mindset. With a positive attitude, we can overcome obstacles, set meaningful goals, and unlock our full potential.

Attitude and Finances

Our attitude towards money and financial matters greatly influences our financial success. A positive attitude towards money fosters a healthy money mindset, encouraging responsible financial habits, and promoting wealth-building behaviors. It helps us make sound financial decisions, manage money effectively, and create a secure financial future. Conversely, a negative attitude towards money can lead to poor financial choices, overspending, and financial stress. By developing a positive attitude towards finances, we can achieve financial independence and stability.

Attitude and Education

Attitude plays a significant role in our educational journey. A positive attitude towards learning enhances motivation, engagement, and academic performance. It enables us to embrace challenges, persist in the face of difficulties, and seek opportunities for growth. A positive attitude also fosters a love for learning, curiosity, and a thirst for knowledge. By cultivating a positive attitude towards education, we can maximize our learning potential and achieve academic success.

Attitude and Parenting

Attitude is crucial in parenting and shaping the parent-child relationship. A positive attitude towards parenting promotes effective communication, empathy, and understanding. It helps parents create a nurturing and supportive environment for their children, fostering their emotional well-being and resilience. A positive attitude also encourages positive discipline techniques, teaching children valuable life skills and promoting their overall development. By nurturing a positive attitude in parenting, we can raise confident, resilient, and well-adjusted children.

Attitude and Social Interactions

Our attitude towards others greatly influences our social interactions. A positive attitude fosters empathy, kindness, and understanding, enabling us to build meaningful connections with others. It promotes cultural sensitivity, respect for diversity, and inclusive behaviors. A positive attitude also contributes to a positive social environment, where cooperation, collaboration, and mutual support thrive. By cultivating a positive attitude in our social interactions, we can create a harmonious and inclusive society.

Attitude and Personal Happiness

Attitude is a fundamental factor in personal happiness. A positive attitude allows us to appreciate the present moment, find joy in everyday experiences, and maintain a sense of gratitude. It enables us to focus on the positives, even in challenging times, and develop a resilient mindset. A positive attitude also promotes mindfulness, self-care, and emotional well-being. By cultivating a positive attitude, we can enhance our overall happiness and lead a more fulfilling life.

Attitude and Overcoming Challenges

Attitude plays a crucial role in overcoming challenges and adversity. A positive attitude empowers us to face difficulties with resilience, determination, and a problem-solving mindset. It enables us to view challenges as opportunities for growth and learning, rather than insurmountable obstacles. A positive attitude also helps us manage fear, embrace change, and adapt to new situations. By developing a positive attitude, we can navigate life's challenges with grace and emerge stronger on the other side.

In conclusion, attitude intelligence is essential in every aspect of life. Our attitude shapes our experiences, influences our relationships, impacts our career success, affects our health and well-being, drives personal development, shapes our financial outcomes, influences our educational journey, impacts our parenting approach, shapes our social interactions, contributes to personal happiness, and empowers us to overcome challenges. By developing and nurturing a positive attitude, we can unlock our full potential, lead a more fulfilling life, and inspire others to do the same.

1.3 The Power of Positive Attitude

A positive attitude is a powerful tool that can greatly impact every aspect of our lives. Attitude intelligence, the ability to understand and manage our attitudes, plays a crucial role in determining our overall well-being and success. When we cultivate a positive attitude, we open ourselves up to a world of possibilities and create a foundation for personal growth and happiness.

The Impact of Attitude on Our Thoughts and Actions

Our attitude shapes our thoughts and actions, influencing how we perceive and respond to the world around us. A positive attitude allows us to approach challenges with optimism and resilience, enabling us to overcome obstacles and find solutions. It helps us maintain a growth mindset, where we see failures as opportunities for learning and growth rather than setbacks.

On the other hand, a negative attitude can hinder our progress and limit our potential. It can lead to self-doubt, fear, and a lack of motivation. Negative attitudes can also affect our relationships, as they can create barriers to effective communication and hinder our ability to connect with others.

The Power of Positive Thinking

Positive thinking is a key component of a positive attitude. It involves focusing on the good in any situation and maintaining an optimistic outlook. When we practice positive thinking, we train our minds to see the possibilities and opportunities that exist, even in challenging circumstances.

Research has shown that positive thinking can have a profound impact on our mental and physical well-being. It can reduce stress levels, improve our immune system, and enhance our overall resilience. Positive thinking also helps us build stronger relationships, as it fosters empathy, understanding, and effective communication.

The Benefits of a Positive Attitude

A positive attitude brings numerous benefits to our lives. Here are some of the ways it can positively impact different aspects of our lives:

Personal Relationships

A positive attitude is essential for building and maintaining healthy relationships. It allows us to approach interactions with kindness, empathy, and understanding. When we have a positive attitude, we are more likely to attract positive people into our lives and create a supportive network of friends and loved ones. It also helps us navigate conflicts and challenges in relationships, as we approach them with a solution-oriented mindset and a willingness to compromise.

Professional Life

In the workplace, a positive attitude can significantly impact our career success. Employers value employees who bring a positive energy to the workplace, as it fosters a productive and harmonious work environment. A positive attitude also enhances our problem-solving skills, creativity, and ability to adapt to change. It can open doors to new opportunities and help us build strong professional networks.

Health and Well-being

Our attitude has a direct impact on our physical and mental health. A positive attitude can boost our immune system, reduce stress levels, and improve our overall well-being. It helps us cope with challenges and setbacks, promoting emotional resilience. Additionally, a positive attitude encourages healthy habits such as regular exercise, proper nutrition, and self-care, leading to better physical health.

Personal Development

A positive attitude is crucial for personal growth and development. It allows us to set and achieve goals, as we believe in our abilities and maintain a determined mindset. A positive attitude also fosters self-confidence, enabling us to step out of our comfort zones and embrace new experiences. It encourages continuous learning and self-improvement, as we approach challenges with a mindset of curiosity and growth.

Happiness and Well-being

Ultimately, a positive attitude is a key ingredient for personal happiness. When we maintain a positive outlook on life, we are more likely to experience joy, gratitude, and contentment. A positive attitude helps us appreciate the present moment and find beauty in the simple things. It allows us to let go of negativity and focus on the things that truly matter, leading to a more fulfilling and meaningful life.

Cultivating a Positive Attitude

Cultivating a positive attitude is a lifelong journey that requires self-awareness and intentional effort. Here are some strategies to help develop and maintain a positive attitude:

1. Practice gratitude: Take time each day to reflect on the things you are grateful for. This simple practice can shift your focus towards the positive aspects of your life.
2. Surround yourself with positivity: Surround yourself with positive people who uplift and inspire you. Limit exposure to negative influences, such as excessive news consumption or toxic relationships.
3. Challenge negative thoughts: When negative thoughts arise, challenge them with positive affirmations and counter them with evidence of positive experiences.
4. Practice self-care: Take care of your physical, mental, and emotional well-being. Engage in activities that bring you joy and relaxation, such as exercise, meditation, or hobbies.
5. Seek support: Reach out to friends, family, or professionals for support when needed. Building a strong support system can help you navigate challenges and maintain a positive attitude.

Remember, developing a positive attitude takes time and effort. Be patient with yourself and celebrate small victories along the way. With practice and perseverance, you can harness the power of a positive attitude and transform your life in remarkable ways.

1.4 Developing Attitude Intelligence

Developing Attitude Intelligence is a crucial step towards achieving success and happiness in every aspect of life. Attitude Intelligence refers to the ability to understand, manage, and cultivate a positive attitude in various situations. It involves being aware of one's thoughts, emotions, and behaviors, and consciously choosing to adopt a positive mindset.

The Importance of Developing Attitude Intelligence

Attitude Intelligence plays a significant role in shaping our lives and influencing the outcomes we experience. It affects our relationships, career, health, personal development, financial success, education, parenting, social interactions, and overall happiness. By developing Attitude Intelligence, we can enhance our ability to navigate through challenges, overcome obstacles, and make the most out of every situation.

Understanding Attitude Intelligence

Before we delve into the process of developing Attitude Intelligence, it is essential to understand its core components. Attitude Intelligence comprises self-awareness, emotional intelligence, resilience, adaptability, and a growth mindset.

Self-awareness involves recognizing and understanding our thoughts, emotions, and behaviors. It allows us to identify patterns, triggers, and areas for improvement. By being self-aware, we can consciously choose our attitudes and responses in different situations.

Emotional intelligence is the ability to recognize, understand, and manage our emotions and the emotions of others. It enables us to empathize, communicate effectively, and build strong relationships. Emotional intelligence is closely linked to Attitude Intelligence as it helps us regulate our emotions and maintain a positive attitude.

Resilience is the capacity to bounce back from setbacks, adapt to change, and maintain a positive attitude in the face of adversity. Developing resilience is crucial for building Attitude Intelligence as it allows us to view challenges as opportunities for growth and learning.

Adaptability refers to the ability to adjust and thrive in different environments and circumstances. It involves being open-minded, flexible, and willing to embrace change. Developing adaptability is essential for cultivating Attitude Intelligence as it enables us to approach situations with a positive and proactive mindset.

A growth mindset is the belief that our abilities and intelligence can be developed through dedication and hard work. It involves embracing challenges, persisting in the face of obstacles, and seeing failures as opportunities for growth. Cultivating a growth mindset is fundamental to developing Attitude Intelligence as it fosters a positive and optimistic outlook on life.

Strategies for Developing Attitude Intelligence

Developing Attitude Intelligence is an ongoing process that requires conscious effort and practice. Here are some strategies to help you cultivate and enhance your Attitude Intelligence:

1. Self-reflection: Take time to reflect on your thoughts, emotions, and behaviors. Identify any negative patterns or attitudes that may be holding you back. Challenge and reframe negative thoughts into positive ones.

2. Mindfulness: Practice mindfulness to increase self-awareness and focus on the present moment. Mindfulness allows you to observe your thoughts and emotions without judgment, enabling you to choose a positive attitude.

3. Emotional regulation: Learn to recognize and manage your emotions effectively. Practice techniques such as deep breathing, meditation, and journaling to regulate your emotions and maintain a positive attitude.

4. Surround yourself with positivity: Surround yourself with positive people, environments, and influences. Engage in activities that bring you joy and inspire positivity. Limit exposure to negative news, social media, and toxic

relationships.

5. Continuous learning: Cultivate a thirst for knowledge and personal growth. Embrace challenges and seek opportunities to learn and develop new skills. Adopt a growth mindset that views failures as stepping stones to success.

6. Practice gratitude: Cultivate a habit of gratitude by regularly expressing appreciation for the blessings in your life. Focus on the positive aspects of each day and maintain a gratitude journal to remind yourself of the good things.

7. Set goals: Set clear and achievable goals that align with your values and aspirations. Break them down into smaller, manageable steps and celebrate your progress along the way. Goal setting provides direction and motivation, fostering a positive attitude.

8. Seek support: Surround yourself with a supportive network of friends, family, or mentors who can provide guidance and encouragement. Share your goals and aspirations with them, and seek their feedback and support.

9. Embrace failure and learn from it: View failures as opportunities for growth and learning. Analyze your failures, identify lessons learned, and use them to improve and develop a more positive attitude.

10. Practice self-care: Take care of your physical, mental, and emotional well-being. Prioritize activities that promote relaxation, stress reduction, and self-care. Engage in regular exercise, get enough sleep, and nourish your body with healthy food.

By implementing these strategies and committing to the development of Attitude Intelligence, you can transform your mindset and approach to life. Remember, developing Attitude Intelligence is a lifelong journey that requires consistent effort and practice. Embrace the process, be patient with yourself, and celebrate the progress you make along the way.

Chapter 2

Attitude Intelligence in Personal Relationships

2.1 Attitude and Communication
Communication is a fundamental aspect of human interaction, and it plays a crucial role in personal relationships. The way we communicate with others can greatly impact the quality of our relationships and the overall dynamics within them. Attitude intelligence, which refers to the ability to understand and manage one's attitude effectively, is essential in fostering healthy and meaningful communication.

Attitude intelligence in communication involves being aware of our own attitudes and emotions, as well as being sensitive to the attitudes and emotions of others. It requires us to approach conversations with an open mind, empathy, and a willingness to listen and understand. When we possess a positive attitude, it becomes easier to communicate effectively and build strong connections with others.

One of the key elements of attitude intelligence in communication is self-awareness. By being aware of our own attitudes, beliefs, and emotions, we can better understand how they may influence our communication style. For example, if we have a negative attitude or are feeling stressed, it may affect the way we express ourselves and how we interpret the words and actions of others. Being mindful of our own attitudes allows us to regulate our emotions and choose our words more carefully, leading to more constructive and positive communication.

Empathy is another crucial aspect of attitude intelligence in communication. It involves putting ourselves in the shoes of others and trying to understand their perspectives, feelings, and needs. When we approach communication with empathy, we create a safe and supportive environment where individuals feel heard and valued. By actively listening and acknowledging the emotions of others, we can foster deeper connections and build trust in our relationships.

Attitude intelligence also involves effective verbal and non-verbal communication skills. Verbal communication includes the words we choose, the tone of our voice, and the clarity of our message. It is important to express ourselves clearly and respectfully, using language that is inclusive and non-judgmental. Non-verbal communication, on the other hand, includes body language, facial expressions, and gestures. Being aware of our non-verbal cues and understanding how they may be perceived by others is essential in maintaining positive and effective communication.

In addition to self-awareness, empathy, and effective communication skills, attitude intelligence in communication also requires active listening. Active listening involves giving our full attention to the speaker, without interrupting or judging. It involves not only hearing the words being spoken but also understanding the underlying emotions and intentions. By actively listening, we show respect and validate the speaker's experiences, which can lead to more meaningful and productive conversations.

Attitude intelligence in communication also involves the ability to manage conflicts and disagreements in a constructive manner. Conflicts are a natural part of any relationship, but how we approach and resolve them can greatly impact the overall dynamics. With a positive attitude, we can approach conflicts with a problem-solving mindset, seeking common ground and understanding. By focusing on finding solutions rather than blaming or criticizing, we can maintain open lines of communication and strengthen our relationships.

In conclusion, attitude intelligence plays a vital role in communication within personal relationships. By being self-aware, empathetic, and possessing effective communication skills, we can foster healthy and meaningful connections with others. Active listening, managing conflicts constructively, and maintaining a positive attitude are all essential components of attitude intelligence in communication. By continuously developing our attitude intelligence, we can enhance the quality of our relationships and create a more harmonious and fulfilling life.

2.2 Building Healthy Relationships

Building healthy relationships is a fundamental aspect of our lives. Whether it's with our family, friends, romantic partners, or colleagues, the quality of our relationships greatly impacts our overall well-being and happiness. Attitude intelligence plays a crucial role in fostering and maintaining these relationships.

The Foundation of Healthy Relationships

At the core of building healthy relationships is having a positive attitude towards others. This involves approaching interactions with kindness, empathy, and respect. When we have a positive attitude, we are more likely to create an environment of trust and understanding, which forms the foundation of strong and lasting relationships.

Effective Communication

Communication is a key component of any relationship, and attitude intelligence plays a vital role in ensuring effective communication. When we approach conversations with a positive attitude, we are more open-minded, receptive, and willing to listen to others. This allows for better understanding and prevents misunderstandings or conflicts from arising.

Attitude intelligence also involves being aware of our own emotions and how they may impact our communication. By managing our emotions and responding in a calm and respectful manner, we can avoid unnecessary arguments and maintain healthy dialogue.

Empathy and Understanding

Empathy is the ability to understand and share the feelings of others. It is a crucial aspect of building healthy relationships. Attitude intelligence helps us develop empathy by encouraging us to put ourselves in the shoes of others and consider their perspectives and experiences.

When we approach relationships with empathy, we are better able to understand the needs and emotions of others. This allows us to respond in a supportive and compassionate manner, strengthening the bond between individuals.

Trust and Reliability

Trust is the cornerstone of any healthy relationship. Attitude intelligence helps us build trust by consistently demonstrating reliability, honesty, and integrity. When we have a positive attitude towards others, we are more likely to follow through on our commitments, be transparent in our actions, and maintain confidentiality when necessary.

By consistently displaying trustworthiness, we create an environment where others feel safe and secure in sharing their thoughts, feelings, and vulnerabilities. This fosters deeper connections and strengthens the overall relationship.

Conflict Resolution

No relationship is without its conflicts or disagreements. However, attitude intelligence equips us with the skills to navigate these challenges in a constructive and respectful manner. When conflicts arise, having a positive attitude allows us to approach them with a mindset of finding a solution rather than placing blame.

Attitude intelligence encourages active listening, empathy, and compromise during conflict resolution. It helps us focus on understanding the underlying issues and finding mutually beneficial resolutions. By approaching conflicts with a positive attitude, we can preserve the relationship and even strengthen it through the process of resolving differences.

Building and Maintaining Positivity

Attitude intelligence emphasizes the importance of maintaining a positive attitude in relationships. Positivity not only enhances our own well-being but also has a contagious effect on those around us. When we approach relationships with optimism and positivity, we create an uplifting and supportive environment.

Building and maintaining positivity involves expressing gratitude, offering compliments, and celebrating the successes of others. It also means reframing challenges as opportunities for growth and maintaining a hopeful outlook even during difficult times. By cultivating a positive attitude, we contribute to the overall happiness and satisfaction within our relationships.

Conclusion

Building healthy relationships is a lifelong journey that requires continuous effort and growth. Attitude intelligence plays a vital role in this process by guiding our interactions with kindness, empathy, and respect. By developing a positive attitude towards others, practicing effective communication, fostering empathy, building trust, resolving conflicts constructively, and maintaining positivity, we can create and nurture strong and fulfilling relationships in every aspect of our lives.

2.3 Resolving Conflicts with Attitude Intelligence

Conflict is an inevitable part of life, and it can arise in various aspects of our personal relationships. Whether it's with our partners, family members, friends, or colleagues, conflicts can be challenging and emotionally draining. However, with the application of Attitude Intelligence, we can effectively resolve conflicts and maintain healthy relationships.

Resolving conflicts requires a combination of emotional intelligence, effective communication, and a positive attitude. Attitude Intelligence plays a crucial role in conflict resolution as it helps us approach conflicts with empathy, understanding, and a willingness to find mutually beneficial solutions. Here are some key strategies for resolving conflicts with Attitude Intelligence:

1. Self-awareness and self-regulation

Before attempting to resolve a conflict, it is essential to be aware of our own emotions, biases, and triggers. Self-awareness allows us to understand how our attitudes and beliefs may influence the conflict. By recognizing our emotional state, we can regulate our reactions and respond to the conflict in a calm and composed manner. This self-regulation helps create a positive environment for conflict resolution.

2. Active listening

Effective communication is the cornerstone of conflict resolution. Active listening involves giving our full attention to the other person, understanding their perspective, and validating their feelings. By actively listening, we demonstrate respect and empathy, which can help de-escalate the conflict and foster a collaborative atmosphere. It is important to avoid interrupting or formulating responses while the other person is speaking, as this can hinder effective communication.

3. Empathy and understanding

Empathy is the ability to understand and share the feelings of another person. By putting ourselves in the other person's shoes, we can gain a deeper understanding of their perspective and motivations. This understanding allows us to approach the conflict with compassion and find common ground. It is important to remember that empathy does not mean agreement, but rather a willingness to acknowledge and validate the other person's emotions and experiences.

4. Collaborative problem-solving

Conflict resolution should aim for win-win solutions, where both parties feel heard and their needs are met. Collaborative problem-solving involves brainstorming ideas, considering different perspectives, and finding creative solutions that address the underlying issues. By focusing on common goals and shared interests, we can work together to find mutually beneficial outcomes. It is important to approach the conflict with a mindset of cooperation rather than competition.

5. Maintaining a positive attitude

A positive attitude is crucial during conflict resolution, as it helps create a constructive and supportive environment. By maintaining a positive mindset, we can approach the conflict as an opportunity for growth and learning. It is important to avoid blame, criticism, and negative language, as these can escalate the conflict and hinder resolution. Instead, focus on finding solutions and expressing appreciation for the other person's willingness to engage in the resolution process.

6. Seeking professional help if needed

In some cases, conflicts may be deeply rooted or complex, requiring the assistance of a trained professional, such as a mediator or therapist. Seeking professional help does not indicate weakness but rather a commitment to finding a resolution that is fair and beneficial for all parties involved. A neutral third party can provide guidance, facilitate communication, and help navigate through challenging emotions.

Resolving conflicts with Attitude Intelligence requires patience, understanding, and a genuine desire to find common ground. It is important to remember that conflicts are opportunities for growth and strengthening relationships. By applying the principles of Attitude Intelligence, we can transform conflicts into opportunities for personal and interpersonal development.

2.4 Maintaining Positive Attitude in Relationships

Maintaining a positive attitude in relationships is crucial for fostering healthy and fulfilling connections with others. Whether it's a romantic partnership, a friendship, or a professional relationship, the way we approach and maintain our attitude can significantly impact the dynamics and outcomes of these interactions. In this section, we will explore the importance of maintaining a positive attitude in relationships and provide practical strategies for cultivating and sustaining it.

The Power of a Positive Attitude in Relationships

A positive attitude is like a magnet that attracts positivity and fosters harmonious relationships. When we approach our relationships with optimism, kindness, and empathy, we create an environment that is conducive to growth, understanding, and mutual support. A positive attitude allows us to see the best in others, appreciate their strengths, and forgive their shortcomings. It helps us navigate conflicts with grace and find solutions that benefit both parties involved.

The Challenges of Maintaining a Positive Attitude

Maintaining a positive attitude in relationships can be challenging, especially when faced with disagreements, misunderstandings, or difficult circumstances. It's natural to experience moments of frustration, disappointment, or anger. However, it's essential to recognize that our attitude is within our control, and we have the power to choose how we respond to these challenges.

Strategies for Maintaining a Positive Attitude

1. **Practice Self-Awareness**: Developing self-awareness is the first step towards maintaining a positive attitude in relationships. Take the time to reflect on your thoughts, emotions, and reactions. Notice any negative patterns or biases that may be influencing your attitude. By understanding yourself better, you can consciously choose to respond in a more positive and constructive manner.

2. **Choose Empathy**: Empathy is the ability to understand and share the feelings of others. When we approach relationships with empathy, we can better understand the perspectives and emotions of those around us. This understanding allows us to respond with compassion and kindness, even in challenging situations. Practice active listening, put yourself in the other person's shoes, and validate their feelings and experiences.

3. **Focus on the Positive**: It's easy to get caught up in negativity and dwell on the flaws or mistakes of others. Instead, make a conscious effort to focus on the positive aspects of your relationships. Express gratitude for the qualities you appreciate in the other person and acknowledge their efforts. Celebrate their successes and strengths, and let them know that you value and cherish their presence in your life.

4. **Communicate Effectively**: Effective communication is vital for maintaining positive relationships. Be mindful of your tone, body language, and choice of words. Practice active listening and strive to understand the other person's perspective before responding. Avoid making assumptions or jumping to conclusions. Instead, ask clarifying questions and seek mutual understanding. Clear and respectful communication can prevent misunderstandings and foster a positive atmosphere.

5. **Practice Forgiveness**: Holding onto grudges or past grievances can poison relationships and hinder personal

growth. Learn to forgive and let go of resentment. Understand that everyone makes mistakes, and holding onto anger only harms yourself and the relationship. Forgiveness allows for healing and creates space for growth and positive change.

6. **Take Responsibility**: Maintaining a positive attitude also means taking responsibility for your actions and emotions. Acknowledge your role in conflicts or misunderstandings and be willing to apologize when necessary. Avoid blaming others or playing the victim. By taking responsibility, you empower yourself to make positive changes and contribute to the growth of the relationship.

7. **Cultivate Self-Care**: Taking care of your own well-being is essential for maintaining a positive attitude in relationships. Engage in activities that bring you joy and fulfillment. Prioritize self-care practices such as exercise, meditation, and spending time with loved ones. When you take care of yourself, you are better equipped to show up with a positive attitude in your relationships.

Conclusion

Maintaining a positive attitude in relationships is a continuous practice that requires self-awareness, empathy, effective communication, forgiveness, and personal responsibility. By cultivating a positive attitude, we create an environment that nurtures healthy and fulfilling connections with others. Remember, your attitude is within your control, and by choosing positivity, you can enhance the quality of your relationships and bring joy and fulfillment into your life.

Chapter 3

Attitude Intelligence in Professional Life

3.1 Attitude and Career Success

Having a positive attitude is not only important for personal well-being but also plays a crucial role in achieving career success. Attitude intelligence, the ability to understand and manage one's attitude, can significantly impact an individual's professional growth and advancement. In this section, we will explore the connection between attitude and career success and discuss strategies for developing a winning attitude at work.

The Power of Attitude in the Workplace

Attitude is a powerful force that can shape the work environment and influence the outcomes of our professional endeavors. A positive attitude can inspire and motivate colleagues, foster teamwork, and enhance productivity. On the other hand, a negative attitude can create a toxic work environment, hinder collaboration, and impede progress.

Employers value individuals with a positive attitude because they bring enthusiasm, resilience, and a can-do mindset to their work. They are more likely to take initiative, embrace challenges, and find creative solutions to problems. Moreover, a positive attitude can help individuals navigate through setbacks and failures, enabling them to bounce back stronger and more determined.

Attitude and Career Advancement

Attitude plays a crucial role in career advancement. Employers not only look for individuals with the right skills and qualifications but also those who possess the right attitude. A positive attitude can set individuals apart from their peers and open doors to new opportunities.

One of the key aspects of attitude intelligence in the workplace is maintaining a growth mindset. Embracing a growth mindset means believing in one's ability to learn and grow, even in the face of challenges and setbacks. Individuals with a growth mindset are more likely to seek out new experiences, take on challenging projects, and continuously develop their skills. This mindset not only enhances personal growth but also demonstrates to employers a willingness to adapt and improve.

Developing a Winning Attitude at Work

Developing a winning attitude at work requires self-awareness, self-reflection, and a commitment to personal growth. Here are some strategies to cultivate a positive attitude and increase your chances of career success:

1. Cultivate a Positive Mindset

Start by cultivating a positive mindset. Focus on the opportunities rather than the obstacles, and approach challenges with a solution-oriented mindset. Train yourself to see setbacks as learning experiences and opportunities for growth. Surround yourself with positive influences, whether it be supportive colleagues, inspiring mentors, or motivational resources.

2. Set Clear Goals

Setting clear goals is essential for maintaining a positive attitude at work. When you have a clear vision of what you want to achieve, it becomes easier to stay motivated and focused. Break down your goals into smaller, manageable tasks, and celebrate your achievements along the way. This will help you maintain a positive attitude and stay motivated, even during challenging times.

3. Practice Self-Reflection

Regular self-reflection is crucial for developing attitude intelligence. Take the time to assess your attitudes and beliefs about work, success, and challenges. Identify any negative thought patterns or limiting beliefs that may be holding you back. Replace them with positive affirmations and empowering beliefs that support your career growth.

4. Embrace Continuous Learning

Embrace a mindset of continuous learning and professional development. Stay updated with industry trends, seek out new learning opportunities, and invest in your skills and knowledge. This not only enhances your expertise but also demonstrates your commitment to personal growth and improvement.

5. Foster Positive Relationships

Build positive relationships with your colleagues and superiors. Cultivate a supportive and collaborative work environment by offering help, showing appreciation, and practicing effective communication. Surrounding yourself with positive and like-minded individuals can significantly impact your attitude and overall job satisfaction.

6. PRACTICE RESILIENCE

Resilience is the ability to bounce back from setbacks and adapt to change. Cultivate resilience by reframing failures as learning opportunities, seeking feedback, and developing coping mechanisms for stress. Resilient individuals are better equipped to handle challenges and maintain a positive attitude in the face of adversity.

7. Take Ownership of Your Attitude

Remember that your attitude is within your control. Take ownership of your attitude and consciously choose to approach work with a positive mindset. Avoid blaming external factors for your attitude and instead focus on developing the resilience and adaptability needed to thrive in any situation.

By developing attitude intelligence and cultivating a positive attitude, you can enhance your career success and create a fulfilling and rewarding professional life. Remember, attitude is not just a reflection of your current circumstances; it is a powerful tool that can shape your future. Embrace the power of attitude and unlock your full potential in the workplace.

3.2 Developing a Winning Attitude at Work

In today's competitive and fast-paced work environment, having a winning attitude is crucial for success. Your attitude at work not only affects your own performance and job satisfaction but also has a significant impact on your colleagues, team dynamics, and overall organizational culture. Developing a winning attitude at work is about cultivating a positive mindset, embracing challenges, and consistently striving for excellence. In this section, we will explore the key elements of developing a winning attitude and how it can contribute to your professional growth and success.

The Power of a Positive Attitude

A positive attitude is the foundation of a winning mindset. It is the belief that you can overcome obstacles, learn from failures, and achieve your goals. When you approach your work with a positive attitude, you become more resilient, adaptable, and open to new opportunities. Your enthusiasm and optimism can inspire and motivate others, creating a positive work environment that fosters collaboration and innovation.

To develop a positive attitude, start by focusing on the things you can control. Instead of dwelling on problems or setbacks, shift your mindset towards finding solutions and learning from the experience. Practice gratitude by acknowledging and appreciating the positive aspects of your work and the contributions of your colleagues. Surround yourself with positive and supportive individuals who uplift and encourage you.

Embracing Challenges and Growth Opportunities

A winning attitude involves embracing challenges and viewing them as opportunities for growth. Instead of shying away from difficult tasks or projects, approach them with a mindset of curiosity and a willingness to learn. Recognize that challenges provide valuable learning experiences and can lead to personal and professional development.

To develop a winning attitude towards challenges, adopt a growth mindset. Embrace the belief that your abilities and intelligence can be developed through dedication and hard work. Emphasize the process of learning and improvement rather than focusing solely on the outcome. Seek feedback from others and use it as a tool for self-reflection and growth. By embracing challenges and continuously seeking opportunities to learn and improve, you will develop the resilience and determination necessary for success.

Setting Goals and Maintaining Focus

A winning attitude at work involves setting clear goals and maintaining focus on achieving them. Goals provide direction and purpose, helping you stay motivated and committed to your work. When setting goals, ensure they are specific, measurable, attainable, relevant, and time-bound (SMART). This will help you stay focused and track your progress.

To develop a winning attitude towards goal setting, break down your goals into smaller, manageable tasks. This will make them less overwhelming and increase your chances of success. Prioritize your tasks based on their importance and urgency, and allocate your time and resources accordingly. Regularly review and adjust your goals as needed to ensure they align with your evolving priorities and aspirations.

Cultivating a Strong Work Ethic

A winning attitude at work is closely tied to having a strong work ethic. It involves being diligent, reliable, and committed to delivering high-quality work. Cultivating a strong work ethic means taking ownership of your responsibilities, meeting deadlines, and going above and beyond what is expected of you.

To develop a winning attitude towards work ethic, strive for excellence in everything you do. Take pride in your work and consistently seek ways to improve and exceed expectations. Be proactive and take initiative, anticipating and addressing challenges before they arise. Demonstrate reliability and dependability by consistently delivering on your commitments. By cultivating a strong work ethic, you not only enhance your own professional reputation but also contribute to a positive and productive work environment.

Building Positive Relationships and Collaboration

A winning attitude at work extends beyond individual performance. It involves building positive relationships and fostering collaboration with colleagues and team members. Recognize that success is often a collective effort, and by working together, you can achieve greater outcomes.

To develop a winning attitude towards building positive relationships, practice effective communication and active listening. Be respectful and supportive of your colleagues' ideas and contributions. Offer help and support when needed and be willing to collaborate and share credit for achievements. Foster a sense of camaraderie and teamwork by celebrating successes and acknowledging the efforts of others. By building positive relationships and fostering collaboration, you create a supportive and inclusive work environment that promotes productivity and success.

In conclusion, developing a winning attitude at work is essential for professional growth and success. By cultivating a positive mindset, embracing challenges, setting goals, maintaining focus, cultivating a strong work ethic, and building positive relationships, you can create a winning attitude that not only benefits you but also contributes to a positive and productive work environment. Remember, your attitude is within your control, and by consciously choosing to develop a winning attitude, you can unlock your full potential and achieve greater success in your professional life.

3.3 Leadership and Attitude Intelligence

Leadership is a crucial aspect of professional life, and it plays a significant role in the success of individuals and organizations. Effective leaders possess a unique set of skills and qualities that enable them to inspire and motivate their teams. One such quality that distinguishes exceptional leaders is their attitude intelligence.

Attitude intelligence in leadership refers to the ability to understand and manage one's own attitude while also influencing the attitudes of others in a positive and constructive manner. It involves being aware of the impact of one's attitude on team dynamics, decision-making, and overall organizational culture. Leaders with high attitude intelligence are able to create an environment that fosters collaboration, innovation, and growth.

The Role of Attitude Intelligence in Leadership

Leadership is not just about giving orders and making decisions; it is about inspiring and guiding others towards a common goal. Attitude intelligence plays a crucial role in effective leadership by influencing how leaders interact with their team members and how they approach challenges and opportunities.

1. **Building Trust and Rapport:** Leaders with high attitude intelligence understand the importance of building trust and rapport with their team members. They recognize that a positive attitude is contagious and can create a sense of trust and loyalty among team members. By demonstrating a positive and optimistic attitude, leaders can inspire confidence in their abilities and create a supportive and collaborative work environment.

2. **Motivating and Inspiring:** Attitude intelligence enables leaders to motivate and inspire their team members. Leaders who possess a positive attitude are more likely to inspire their team members to go above and beyond their regular duties. They can effectively communicate their vision, set clear goals, and provide the necessary support and encouragement to help their team members achieve their full potential.

3. **Resilience and Adaptability:** Leaders face numerous challenges and setbacks in their roles. Attitude intelligence helps leaders develop resilience and adaptability in the face of adversity. Leaders with a positive attitude are better equipped to handle setbacks, learn from failures, and find creative solutions to problems. They can inspire their team members to embrace change and adapt to new situations with a positive mindset.

4. **Conflict Resolution:** Conflict is inevitable in any team or organization. Leaders with high attitude intelligence are skilled at resolving conflicts in a constructive manner. They

approach conflicts with a positive attitude, seeking to understand different perspectives and find win-win solutions. By promoting open communication and fostering a positive attitude, leaders can create an environment where conflicts are addressed promptly and effectively.

5. **Emotional Intelligence:** Attitude intelligence is closely linked to emotional intelligence, which is the ability to recognize and manage one's own emotions and the emotions of others. Leaders with high emotional intelligence can understand and empathize with the emotions of their team members, which allows them to respond appropriately and provide the necessary support. This ability to connect on an emotional level fosters trust, loyalty, and a positive work environment.

Developing Attitude Intelligence in Leadership

Attitude intelligence is not a fixed trait; it can be developed and enhanced over time. Leaders who are committed to improving their attitude intelligence can take several steps to cultivate this essential quality:

1. **Self-Reflection:** Leaders should engage in regular self-reflection to gain a deeper understanding of their own attitudes and how they impact their leadership style. They can ask themselves questions such as: "What are my default attitudes in different situations?", "How do my attitudes influence my decision-making?", and "How do my attitudes affect the morale and productivity of my team members?"

2. **Seek Feedback:** Leaders should actively seek feedback from their team members, peers, and mentors regarding their attitudes and leadership style. This feedback can provide valuable insights into blind spots and areas for improvement. By creating a culture of open and honest feedback, leaders can

continuously learn and grow.

3. **Practice Mindfulness:** Mindfulness is the practice of being fully present and aware of one's thoughts, emotions, and actions. Leaders can develop attitude intelligence by practicing mindfulness techniques such as meditation, deep breathing, and self-reflection. Mindfulness helps leaders become more aware of their attitudes in the present moment and enables them to respond consciously rather than react impulsively.

4. **Lead by Example:** Leaders must lead by example and demonstrate the attitudes and behaviors they expect from their team members. By consistently displaying a positive attitude, leaders can inspire and motivate their team members to adopt a similar mindset. Leaders should also be transparent and authentic in their communication, fostering an environment of trust and openness.

5. **Continuous Learning:** Attitude intelligence is a lifelong journey of learning and growth. Leaders should invest in their personal and professional development by attending leadership workshops, reading books on leadership and attitude, and seeking opportunities for self-improvement. By continuously learning and expanding their knowledge, leaders can stay ahead of the curve and adapt to changing circumstances.

The Impact of Attitude Intelligence on Leadership Success

Leaders who possess high attitude intelligence are more likely to achieve long-term success in their roles. Their positive attitudes and behaviors create a ripple effect throughout the organization, leading to increased employee engagement, productivity, and overall satisfaction. Additionally, leaders with high attitude intelligence are better equipped to navigate challenges, build strong relationships, and inspire their teams to reach their full potential.

In conclusion, attitude intelligence is a critical aspect of effective leadership. Leaders who possess high attitude intelligence can create a positive work environment, inspire their team members, and navigate challenges with resilience and adaptability. By developing and enhancing their attitude intelligence, leaders can unlock their full potential and drive success in their personal and professional lives.

3.4 Managing Stress and Attitude in the Workplace

In today's fast-paced and competitive work environment, stress has become a common occurrence for many individuals. The demands of work, deadlines, and the pressure to perform can often lead to high levels of stress. However, managing stress effectively is crucial for maintaining a positive attitude and achieving success in the workplace. This section will explore the relationship between stress, attitude, and strategies for managing stress in the workplace.

The Impact of Stress on Attitude

Stress can have a significant impact on an individual's attitude in the workplace. When faced with high levels of stress, it is common for individuals to experience negative emotions such as frustration, irritability, and anxiety. These negative emotions can affect their overall attitude, leading to decreased motivation, productivity, and job satisfaction.

Furthermore, stress can also impact interpersonal relationships in the workplace. When individuals are stressed, they may become more prone to conflicts, misunderstandings, and communication breakdowns. This can create a negative work environment and hinder collaboration and teamwork.

The Role of Attitude in Managing Stress

Attitude plays a crucial role in managing stress effectively. A positive attitude can help individuals cope with stress more effectively and maintain their overall well-being. When individuals have a positive attitude, they are more likely to approach challenges with resilience, optimism, and a problem-solving mindset.

Having a positive attitude also enables individuals to reframe stressful situations and view them as opportunities for growth and learning. Instead of being overwhelmed by stress, individuals with a positive attitude are more likely to see it as a temporary setback and focus on finding solutions.

Strategies for Managing Stress in the Workplace

1. **Identify and Manage Stress Triggers**: The first step in managing stress is to identify the factors that contribute to it. This could include excessive workload, tight deadlines, conflicts with colleagues, or a lack of work-life balance. Once identified, individuals can develop strategies to manage or minimize these stress triggers. This may involve delegating tasks, setting realistic goals, or improving communication with colleagues.

2. **Practice Stress Reduction Techniques**: There are various stress reduction techniques that individuals can incorporate into their daily routine to manage stress effectively. These techniques include deep breathing exercises, meditation, mindfulness, and physical exercise. Taking regular breaks throughout the workday and engaging in activities that

promote relaxation can also help reduce stress levels.

3. **Develop Time Management Skills**: Poor time management can contribute to increased stress levels. By developing effective time management skills, individuals can prioritize tasks, set realistic deadlines, and avoid procrastination. This can help create a sense of control and reduce the feeling of being overwhelmed by work demands.

4. **Seek Support and Build Relationships**: Building a strong support network in the workplace is essential for managing stress. Having colleagues or mentors who can provide guidance, advice, and emotional support can significantly impact an individual's ability to cope with stress. Additionally, fostering positive relationships with colleagues can create a supportive work environment and reduce stress levels.

5. **Maintain a Healthy Work-Life Balance**: Achieving a healthy work-life balance is crucial for managing stress in the workplace. It is essential to set boundaries between work and personal life, prioritize self-care, and engage in activities outside of work that bring joy and relaxation. Taking regular vacations and breaks from work can also help recharge and reduce stress levels.

6. **Practice Positive Self-Talk**: Positive self-talk involves replacing negative thoughts and self-doubt with positive and empowering statements. By reframing negative thoughts and focusing on one's strengths and abilities, individuals can build resilience and maintain a positive attitude even in stressful situations.

7. **Seek Professional Help if Needed**: If stress levels become overwhelming and start to impact an individual's mental and physical well-being, it is important to seek professional help. Mental health professionals can provide guidance, support, and strategies for managing stress effectively.

The Benefits of Managing Stress and Maintaining a Positive Attitude

Managing stress and maintaining a positive attitude in the workplace can have numerous benefits for individuals and organizations. Some of these benefits include:

- Increased productivity and job satisfaction
- Improved physical and mental well-being
- Enhanced interpersonal relationships and teamwork
- Better decision-making and problem-solving abilities
- Higher levels of motivation and engagement
- Reduced absenteeism and turnover rates

By actively managing stress and cultivating a positive attitude, individuals can create a more fulfilling and successful work experience for themselves and contribute to a positive work culture.

In conclusion, managing stress and maintaining a positive attitude in the workplace are essential for personal well-being and professional success. By identifying stress triggers, practicing stress reduction techniques, developing time management skills, seeking support, maintaining work-life balance, practicing positive self-talk, and seeking professional help when needed, individuals can effectively manage stress and cultivate a positive attitude. The benefits of managing stress and maintaining a positive attitude extend beyond the individual, positively impacting the overall work environment and organizational success.

3.5 Attitude Intelligence for Professional Growth

In the fast-paced and competitive world of professional life, having a positive and growth-oriented attitude is crucial for achieving success and personal growth. Attitude intelligence plays a significant role in shaping our professional journey, influencing our career choices, and determining our level of satisfaction and fulfillment in the workplace. This section will explore the various ways in which attitude intelligence can contribute to professional growth and development.

The Power of a Positive Attitude

A positive attitude is a powerful tool that can significantly impact our professional growth. It not only affects our own mindset and behavior but also influences how others perceive and interact with us. When we approach our work with a positive attitude, we become more resilient, adaptable, and open to learning and growth opportunities.

A positive attitude enables us to embrace challenges and setbacks as opportunities for learning and improvement. Instead of being discouraged by failures, individuals with a positive attitude view them as stepping stones to success. They are more likely to persevere, seek solutions, and bounce back from setbacks with renewed determination.

Cultivating a Growth Mindset

Attitude intelligence is closely linked to the concept of a growth mindset. A growth mindset is the belief that our abilities and intelligence can be developed through dedication, effort, and continuous learning. Embracing a growth mindset allows us to approach our professional growth with enthusiasm and a willingness to take on new challenges.

Individuals with a growth mindset are not afraid to step out of their comfort zones and try new things. They see failures as opportunities for growth and view feedback as valuable input for improvement. By cultivating a growth mindset, we can unlock our full potential and continuously strive for professional growth and development.

Embracing Continuous Learning

Attitude intelligence encourages us to adopt a lifelong learning mindset. In today's rapidly evolving professional landscape, staying relevant and competitive requires a commitment to continuous learning and skill development. By embracing a mindset of continuous learning, we can enhance our knowledge, acquire new skills, and adapt to changing industry trends.

Continuous learning can take various forms, such as attending workshops, seminars, or conferences, pursuing advanced degrees or certifications, or even engaging in self-directed learning through online resources. By actively seeking out opportunities to learn and grow, we demonstrate our commitment to professional development and position ourselves for future success.

Building Strong Professional Relationships

Attitude intelligence also plays a crucial role in building and nurturing strong professional relationships. Positive attitudes are contagious and can create a harmonious and supportive work environment. When we approach our interactions with colleagues, superiors, and subordinates with respect, empathy, and a positive attitude, we foster trust, collaboration, and effective communication.

Strong professional relationships are essential for professional growth as they provide opportunities for mentorship, networking, and career advancement. By cultivating positive relationships, we can gain valuable insights, expand our professional network, and open doors to new opportunities.

Taking Initiative and Seeking Growth Opportunities

Attitude intelligence encourages individuals to take initiative and actively seek out growth opportunities. Instead of waiting for opportunities to come their way, individuals with attitude intelligence proactively identify areas for improvement and take steps to enhance their skills and knowledge.

Taking initiative can involve volunteering for challenging projects, seeking additional responsibilities, or pursuing professional development opportunities. By demonstrating a proactive attitude, we show our commitment to personal growth and development, which can lead to increased recognition, promotions, and career advancement.

Embracing Change and Adaptability

In today's dynamic and ever-changing professional landscape, adaptability is a crucial skill for professional growth. Attitude intelligence enables individuals to embrace change and view it as an opportunity for growth rather than a threat. By maintaining a flexible and adaptable attitude, we can navigate through uncertainties, embrace new technologies and methodologies, and seize emerging opportunities.

Adaptability also involves being open to feedback and constructive criticism. By actively seeking feedback and using it to improve our performance, we demonstrate our willingness to learn and grow. This openness to feedback and adaptability can contribute significantly to our professional growth and success.

Balancing Ambition and Well-being

Attitude intelligence emphasizes the importance of maintaining a healthy work-life balance. While ambition and drive are essential for professional growth, it is equally important to prioritize our well-being and avoid burnout. Attitude intelligence encourages individuals to set realistic goals, manage their time effectively, and prioritize self-care.

By maintaining a healthy work-life balance, we can sustain our motivation, creativity, and productivity in the long run. Taking care of our physical and mental well-being allows us to bring our best selves to the workplace, make better decisions, and achieve sustainable professional growth.

In conclusion, attitude intelligence is a vital factor in professional growth and development. By cultivating a positive attitude, embracing a growth mindset, continuously learning, building strong relationships, taking initiative, adapting to change, and balancing ambition with well-being, we can unlock our full potential and achieve long-term success in our professional lives. Attitude intelligence is not only beneficial for our individual growth but also contributes to creating a positive and thriving work environment.

3.6 Attitude and Work-Life Balance

Work-life balance is a crucial aspect of our lives that directly impacts our overall well-being and happiness. It refers to the equilibrium between our professional commitments and personal responsibilities, allowing us to effectively manage both areas without feeling overwhelmed or burnt out. Attitude intelligence plays a significant role in achieving and maintaining a healthy work-life balance.

The Importance of Work-Life Balance

In today's fast-paced and competitive world, many individuals find themselves struggling to strike a balance between their work and personal lives. The demands of the modern workplace, coupled with personal obligations, can often lead to stress, fatigue, and a sense of dissatisfaction. It is essential to recognize the significance of work-life balance and its impact on our mental, emotional, and physical well-being.

When we neglect our personal lives in favor of work, we may experience a decline in our relationships, health, and overall happiness. On the other hand, if we neglect our professional responsibilities, it can lead to career stagnation or even jeopardize our job security. Achieving a healthy work-life balance allows us to excel in both areas, leading to increased productivity, job satisfaction, and a fulfilling personal life.

Attitude Intelligence and Work-Life Balance

Attitude intelligence plays a vital role in maintaining a healthy work-life balance. It involves cultivating a positive mindset, adopting effective coping strategies, and developing the ability to prioritize and manage our time efficiently. By harnessing the power of attitude intelligence, we can navigate the challenges of balancing work and personal life with grace and resilience.

1. Cultivating a Positive Attitude

A positive attitude is the foundation of a healthy work-life balance. It enables us to approach challenges with optimism, find joy in our daily activities, and maintain a sense of gratitude. By cultivating a positive attitude, we can create a harmonious environment where work and personal life coexist peacefully.

2. Setting Boundaries

Setting clear boundaries between work and personal life is crucial for maintaining a healthy balance. Attitude intelligence helps us establish these boundaries by recognizing the importance of dedicating time and energy to both aspects of our lives. By setting boundaries, we can avoid overworking, prevent burnout, and ensure that we have ample time for ourselves and our loved ones.

3. Effective Time Management

Attitude intelligence empowers us to manage our time effectively, ensuring that we allocate sufficient time to work and personal commitments. By prioritizing tasks, setting realistic goals, and avoiding procrastination, we can optimize our productivity and create space for leisure, relaxation, and personal growth.

4. Stress Management

Stress is a common factor that can disrupt work-life balance. Attitude intelligence equips us with the tools to manage stress effectively. By adopting stress-reducing techniques such as mindfulness, exercise, and self-care, we can minimize the negative impact of stress on our well-being and maintain a healthy balance between work and personal life.

5. Flexibility and Adaptability

Attitude intelligence encourages flexibility and adaptability in our approach to work and personal life. It helps us embrace change, navigate unexpected challenges, and adjust our priorities accordingly. By being open to new possibilities and finding creative solutions, we can maintain a healthy work-life balance even in the face of unforeseen circumstances.

Strategies for Achieving Work-Life Balance

To achieve work-life balance, it is essential to implement practical strategies that align with attitude intelligence. Here are some strategies to consider:

1. Prioritize self-care: Make time for activities that promote your physical, mental, and emotional well-being, such as exercise, hobbies, and relaxation.

2. Establish boundaries: Clearly define your working hours and personal time, and communicate them effectively to your colleagues, friends, and family.

3. Delegate and ask for support: Learn to delegate tasks at work and seek support from your loved ones to lighten your load and create more time for yourself.

4. Practice effective time management: Use tools and techniques such as to-do lists, calendars, and prioritization methods to manage your time efficiently and avoid unnecessary stress.

5. Disconnect from work: Set aside designated periods to disconnect from work-related activities, such as turning off email notifications or avoiding work-related discussions during personal time.

6. Foster open communication: Maintain open and honest communication with your employer, colleagues, and loved ones about your work-life balance needs and concerns.

7. Embrace flexibility: Embrace flexible work arrangements, if

possible, that allow you to balance your professional and personal commitments more effectively.

8. Regularly evaluate and reassess: Continuously assess your work-life balance and make adjustments as needed. Priorities and circumstances may change, so it's important to regularly reassess and realign your approach.

Remember, achieving work-life balance is an ongoing process that requires conscious effort and commitment. By incorporating attitude intelligence into your daily life and implementing these strategies, you can create a harmonious and fulfilling balance between your work and personal responsibilities.

Chapter 4

Attitude Intelligence in Health and Well-Being

4.1 Attitude and Physical Health

Physical health is a crucial aspect of our overall well-being, and it is influenced by various factors, including our attitude. Attitude intelligence plays a significant role in maintaining and improving our physical health. Our mindset, beliefs, and attitudes towards our bodies, exercise, nutrition, and self-care can greatly impact our physical well-being.

The Mind-Body Connection

The mind and body are interconnected, and our attitudes can have a profound effect on our physical health. Research has shown that negative emotions, such as stress, anxiety, and anger, can contribute to the development of various health problems, including cardiovascular diseases, weakened immune system, and chronic pain. On the other hand, a positive attitude can enhance our physical health and promote overall well-being.

Attitude and Stress

Stress is a common part of life, and how we perceive and respond to it can significantly impact our physical health. When we have a negative attitude towards stress, viewing it as overwhelming and harmful, it can lead to detrimental effects on our body. Chronic stress can weaken our immune system, increase the risk of developing chronic diseases, and negatively affect our sleep patterns.

However, with attitude intelligence, we can change our perspective on stress. By viewing stress as a natural response that can be managed and used as a catalyst for growth, we can reduce its negative impact on our physical health. Adopting a positive attitude towards stress allows us to develop effective coping mechanisms, such as relaxation techniques, exercise, and seeking support from others.

Attitude and Exercise

Exercise is essential for maintaining physical health, and our attitude towards it can greatly influence our motivation and commitment to regular physical activity. A positive attitude towards exercise can make it enjoyable and increase our adherence to a fitness routine. When we approach exercise with enthusiasm and a belief in its benefits, we are more likely to engage in it consistently.

Attitude intelligence also helps us overcome barriers and challenges related to exercise. Instead of viewing physical activity as a chore or something we have to do, we can cultivate a mindset that sees it as an opportunity for personal growth, self-care, and improved well-being. By focusing on the positive outcomes of exercise, such as increased energy, improved mood, and better physical fitness, we can maintain a long-term commitment to our physical health.

Attitude and Nutrition

Our attitude towards nutrition and food choices also plays a significant role in our physical health. A positive attitude towards healthy eating can lead to better food choices and a balanced diet. When we view nutritious foods as nourishing and beneficial for our bodies, we are more likely to incorporate them into our daily meals.

Attitude intelligence helps us develop a healthy relationship with food by promoting mindful eating and self-awareness. By being aware of our attitudes towards food, such as emotional eating or restrictive behaviors, we can make conscious choices that support our physical health. Cultivating a positive attitude towards nutrition involves embracing a balanced approach, enjoying a variety of foods, and practicing moderation.

Attitude and Self-Care

Self-care is an essential aspect of maintaining physical health, and our attitude towards self-care practices can greatly impact their effectiveness. When we prioritize self-care and view it as a necessary investment in our well-being, we are more likely to engage in activities that promote physical health, such as getting enough sleep, practicing relaxation techniques, and taking breaks when needed.

Attitude intelligence helps us overcome any guilt or negative beliefs associated with self-care. By recognizing that self-care is not selfish but rather a vital component of overall health, we can develop a positive attitude towards taking care of ourselves. This positive mindset allows us to make self-care a priority and reap the benefits of improved physical health and well-being.

In conclusion, attitude intelligence plays a crucial role in our physical health. By cultivating a positive attitude towards stress, exercise, nutrition, and self-care, we can enhance our overall well-being. Our attitudes shape our behaviors and choices, and by adopting a mindset that supports physical health, we can lead a healthier and more fulfilling life.

4.2 Mental Well-being and Attitude Intelligence

Mental well-being is a crucial aspect of our overall health and happiness. It encompasses our emotional, psychological, and social well-being, and plays a significant role in how we think, feel, and act. Our mental well-being affects how we handle stress, make decisions, form relationships, and cope with the challenges of life. Attitude intelligence, with its focus on cultivating a positive mindset and outlook, plays a vital role in promoting and maintaining good mental well-being.

Attitude intelligence is the ability to understand, manage, and control our attitudes and emotions in a way that enhances our mental well-being. It involves developing a positive attitude, resilience, and emotional intelligence to navigate through life's ups and downs. By harnessing the power of attitude intelligence, we can improve our mental well-being and lead a more fulfilling and balanced life.

One of the key aspects of attitude intelligence in relation to mental well-being is the ability to cultivate a positive attitude. A positive attitude is characterized by optimism, gratitude, and a belief in one's ability to overcome challenges. It allows us to approach life with a sense of hope and resilience, even in the face of adversity. Research has shown that individuals with a positive attitude are more likely to experience lower levels of stress, anxiety, and depression, and have better overall mental health.

Attitude intelligence also involves developing emotional intelligence, which is the ability to recognize, understand, and manage our own emotions and the emotions of others. Emotional intelligence allows us to navigate through difficult emotions, such as anger, sadness, or fear, in a healthy and constructive manner. By being aware of our emotions and understanding their impact on our mental well-being, we can make conscious choices to respond to challenging situations in a more positive and adaptive way.

Furthermore, attitude intelligence plays a crucial role in building resilience, which is the ability to bounce back from setbacks and adapt to change. Resilience is essential for maintaining good mental well-being, as it helps us cope with stress, overcome obstacles, and recover from difficult experiences. By developing a resilient mindset, we can view challenges as opportunities for growth, learn from failures, and maintain a positive outlook even in the face of adversity.

Attitude intelligence also encompasses self-care and self-compassion, which are essential for maintaining good mental well-being. Taking care of our physical, emotional, and psychological needs is crucial for overall health and happiness. By practicing self-care, such as getting enough sleep, eating nutritious food, engaging in regular exercise, and engaging in activities that bring us joy and relaxation, we can enhance our mental well-being. Additionally, cultivating self-compassion involves treating ourselves with kindness, understanding, and acceptance, especially during times of difficulty or failure. By practicing self-compassion, we can reduce self-criticism, increase self-esteem, and foster a positive attitude towards ourselves.

Attitude intelligence also involves developing effective coping strategies for managing stress and maintaining mental well-being. Stress is a natural part of life, but how we perceive and respond to stress can significantly impact our mental health. By cultivating a positive attitude and developing healthy coping mechanisms, such as practicing mindfulness, engaging in relaxation techniques, seeking social support, and engaging in activities that bring us joy and fulfillment, we can effectively manage stress and promote our mental well-being.

In conclusion, attitude intelligence plays a crucial role in promoting and maintaining good mental well-being. By cultivating a positive attitude, developing emotional intelligence, building resilience, practicing self-care and self-compassion, and developing effective coping strategies, we can enhance our mental well-being and lead a more fulfilling and balanced life. Attitude intelligence empowers us to navigate through life's challenges with grace and optimism, and enables us to build a strong foundation for our mental health and happiness. By prioritizing our mental well-being and investing in the development of our attitude intelligence, we can unlock our full potential and live a life of purpose, fulfillment, and joy.

4.3 Attitude and Emotional Resilience

Emotional resilience is the ability to adapt and bounce back from difficult situations, setbacks, and challenges. It is a crucial aspect of our overall well-being and plays a significant role in our ability to navigate through life's ups and downs. Attitude intelligence, with its focus on cultivating a positive mindset and outlook, is closely intertwined with emotional resilience.

Having a positive attitude can greatly enhance our emotional resilience. When faced with adversity, individuals with a positive attitude are more likely to view challenges as opportunities for growth and learning. They approach difficult situations with a sense of optimism and believe in their ability to overcome obstacles. This mindset allows them to maintain emotional stability and bounce back more quickly from setbacks.

One of the key components of emotional resilience is the ability to manage and regulate our emotions effectively. Attitude intelligence helps us develop this skill by teaching us to be aware of our emotions and choose how we respond to them. Instead of allowing negative emotions to overwhelm us, we can use our positive attitude to reframe the situation and find constructive ways to cope.

A positive attitude also enables us to maintain perspective during challenging times. It helps us focus on the bigger picture and not get caught up in temporary setbacks. By maintaining a positive outlook, we can avoid falling into a cycle of negativity and self-doubt. This resilience allows us to stay motivated and continue moving forward, even when faced with adversity.

Attitude intelligence also plays a crucial role in building our self-confidence, which is essential for emotional resilience. When we have a positive attitude, we believe in ourselves and our abilities. This self-belief gives us the confidence to face challenges head-on and persevere, even when things get tough. It allows us to trust in our own resilience and bounce back from setbacks with renewed determination.

Furthermore, a positive attitude helps us develop effective coping strategies for managing stress and emotional challenges. Instead of dwelling on negative emotions or engaging in unproductive behaviors, individuals with a positive attitude are more likely to seek healthy outlets for their emotions. They may engage in activities such as exercise, meditation, or journaling to process their feelings and maintain emotional balance.

Attitude intelligence also fosters a sense of gratitude and appreciation, which can greatly enhance emotional resilience. When we cultivate a positive attitude, we learn to focus on the positives in our lives and express gratitude for them. This mindset shift allows us to find joy and contentment even in the face of adversity. It helps us maintain a sense of perspective and reminds us of the many blessings we have, which can be a powerful source of emotional strength.

In addition to these individual benefits, a positive attitude and emotional resilience also have a positive impact on our relationships. When we approach interactions with a positive attitude, we are more likely to handle conflicts and disagreements in a constructive manner. We are better able to empathize with others, understand their perspectives, and find common ground. This ability to maintain emotional balance and respond with empathy strengthens our relationships and fosters a supportive and positive social environment.

In conclusion, attitude intelligence and emotional resilience are closely intertwined. A positive attitude enhances our ability to bounce back from setbacks, manage our emotions effectively, and maintain perspective during challenging times. It empowers us to develop effective coping strategies, build self-confidence, and cultivate gratitude. By nurturing our attitude intelligence, we can develop emotional resilience that positively impacts every aspect of our lives, from personal relationships to professional success and overall well-being.

4.4 Cultivating a Positive Attitude for Better Health

A positive attitude is not only beneficial for our mental and emotional well-being but also plays a significant role in our physical health. Cultivating a positive attitude can have a profound impact on our overall health and well-being. In this section, we will explore the connection between attitude intelligence and better health, and discuss strategies to cultivate a positive attitude for improved physical well-being.

The Mind-Body Connection

The mind and body are intricately connected, and our thoughts and emotions can have a direct impact on our physical health. Research has shown that individuals with a positive attitude tend to have better overall health outcomes compared to those with a negative attitude. A positive attitude can boost our immune system, reduce stress levels, and improve our ability to cope with illness and pain.

Stress Reduction

Stress is a common factor in our daily lives, and chronic stress can have detrimental effects on our health. However, maintaining a positive attitude can help reduce stress levels and its negative impact on our bodies. When we approach stressful situations with a positive mindset, we are better equipped to handle them effectively. Positive thinking can help us reframe challenges as opportunities for growth and find solutions instead of dwelling on the problem.

Boosting the Immune System

Our immune system plays a crucial role in protecting us from illnesses and infections. Studies have shown that a positive attitude can enhance the functioning of our immune system, making us less susceptible to diseases. Positive emotions, such as happiness and optimism, can increase the production of antibodies and activate immune cells, strengthening our body's defense mechanisms.

Faster Recovery and Healing

A positive attitude can also contribute to faster recovery and healing. When we maintain a positive mindset, we create an environment that supports healing and promotes the body's natural ability to repair itself. Positive thoughts and emotions can stimulate the release of endorphins, which are natural painkillers, and promote the production of growth factors that aid in tissue repair.

Healthy Lifestyle Choices

Cultivating a positive attitude can also influence our lifestyle choices, leading to better health outcomes. When we have a positive mindset, we are more likely to engage in healthy behaviors such as regular exercise, balanced nutrition, and adequate sleep. These lifestyle choices are essential for maintaining optimal physical health and can significantly impact our overall well-being.

Strategies for Cultivating a Positive Attitude for Better Health

1. Practice Gratitude: Cultivating a sense of gratitude can shift our focus towards the positive aspects of our lives. Take a few moments each day to reflect on the things you are grateful for, whether it's the support of loved ones, good health, or simple pleasures.

2. Positive Self-Talk: Pay attention to your inner dialogue and replace negative self-talk with positive affirmations. Encourage yourself, celebrate your achievements, and remind yourself of your strengths and capabilities.

3. Surround Yourself with Positivity: Surround yourself with positive influences, whether it's supportive friends and family or uplifting books, music, and media. Limit exposure to negativity and seek out sources of inspiration and motivation.

4. Practice Mindfulness: Mindfulness involves being fully present in the moment and non-judgmentally observing our thoughts and emotions. Regular mindfulness practice can help us become aware of negative thought patterns and replace them with positive and constructive ones.

5. Engage in Activities That Bring Joy: Identify activities that bring you joy and make time for them regularly. Engaging in hobbies, spending time in nature, or pursuing creative outlets can boost your mood and overall well-being.

6. Take Care of Your Physical Health: Physical health and mental well-being are closely intertwined. Prioritize self-care by engaging in regular exercise, eating a balanced diet, getting enough sleep, and practicing relaxation techniques such as deep breathing or meditation.

7. Seek Support: Surround yourself with a supportive network of friends, family, or professionals who can provide guidance and encouragement. Sharing your challenges and seeking support can help you maintain a positive attitude during difficult times.

Remember, cultivating a positive attitude is a lifelong journey. It requires consistent effort and practice. By incorporating these strategies into your daily life, you can cultivate a positive attitude that not only enhances your overall well-being but also contributes to better physical health. Embrace the power of attitude intelligence and unlock the potential for a healthier and happier life.

Chapter 5

Attitude Intelligence in Personal Development

5.1 Attitude and Self-Confidence

Self-confidence is a crucial aspect of personal development and plays a significant role in our overall attitude towards life. Attitude intelligence, with its focus on cultivating a positive mindset, can greatly impact our self-confidence levels. In this section, we will explore the relationship between attitude and self-confidence and how developing attitude intelligence can enhance our belief in ourselves.

The Power of Attitude in Building Self-Confidence

Attitude and self-confidence are closely intertwined. Our attitude towards ourselves, our abilities, and our potential shapes our level of self-confidence. A positive attitude allows us to believe in our capabilities, embrace challenges, and persist in the face of setbacks. On the other hand, a negative attitude can undermine our self-confidence, leading to self-doubt and fear of failure.

Attitude intelligence helps us develop a positive mindset by focusing on self-awareness, self-belief, and self-empowerment. By understanding our strengths, acknowledging our weaknesses, and embracing a growth mindset, we can cultivate a strong foundation of self-confidence.

Embracing Self-Acceptance and Self-Love

Attitude intelligence encourages us to practice self-acceptance and self-love, which are essential for building self-confidence. When we accept ourselves for who we are, including our flaws and imperfections, we free ourselves from the burden of comparison and self-judgment. This acceptance allows us to develop a positive attitude towards ourselves, leading to increased self-confidence.

Self-love is another crucial aspect of attitude intelligence. By nurturing a deep sense of love and compassion for ourselves, we build a strong foundation of self-confidence. When we genuinely believe in our worth and value, we approach challenges with a positive attitude, knowing that we are deserving of success and happiness.

Overcoming Self-Limiting Beliefs

Self-limiting beliefs are negative thoughts and beliefs we hold about ourselves that hinder our self-confidence and personal growth. Attitude intelligence helps us identify and challenge these self-limiting beliefs, replacing them with empowering and positive thoughts.

By cultivating a growth mindset, we understand that our abilities and talents can be developed through dedication and effort. This shift in attitude allows us to overcome self-doubt and embrace challenges as opportunities for growth. As we challenge our self-limiting beliefs and replace them with empowering ones, our self-confidence naturally increases.

Setting and Achieving Goals

Goal setting is an integral part of personal development and plays a significant role in building self-confidence. Attitude intelligence emphasizes the importance of setting realistic and achievable goals that align with our values and aspirations. By setting clear goals, we provide ourselves with a sense of direction and purpose, which boosts our self-confidence.

Attitude intelligence also teaches us to approach goal setting with a positive attitude. Instead of focusing solely on the end result, we learn to appreciate the journey and the progress we make along the way. This positive attitude towards goal setting allows us to maintain our self-confidence, even in the face of obstacles and setbacks.

Cultivating a Positive Inner Dialogue

Our inner dialogue, the thoughts and beliefs we have about ourselves, greatly influences our self-confidence. Attitude intelligence encourages us to cultivate a positive inner dialogue by practicing self-affirmation and positive self-talk.

By consciously replacing negative thoughts with positive and empowering ones, we can rewire our mindset and boost our self-confidence. Instead of dwelling on our weaknesses and failures, we focus on our strengths and past successes. This shift in attitude allows us to approach challenges with a sense of self-assurance and belief in our abilities.

Seeking Growth and Continuous Learning

Attitude intelligence recognizes the importance of continuous learning and personal growth in building self-confidence. By embracing a mindset of lifelong learning, we open ourselves up to new experiences, knowledge, and skills. This continuous growth not only expands our capabilities but also enhances our self-confidence.

When we actively seek opportunities to learn and grow, we develop a sense of competence and mastery. This sense of achievement fuels our self-confidence, as we become more confident in our abilities to navigate various aspects of life.

In conclusion, attitude intelligence plays a vital role in developing self-confidence. By cultivating a positive attitude, embracing self-acceptance, challenging self-limiting beliefs, setting and achieving goals, nurturing a positive inner dialogue, and seeking continuous growth, we can enhance our self confidence and approach life with a strong belief in ourselves. Developing attitude intelligence is a lifelong journey that empowers us to overcome challenges, embrace opportunities, and live a fulfilling and confident life.

5.2 Goal Setting and Attitude Intelligence

Goal setting is an essential aspect of personal development and achievement. It provides direction, motivation, and a sense of purpose in life. When combined with attitude intelligence, goal setting becomes even more powerful and effective. Attitude intelligence is the ability to cultivate a positive mindset, overcome obstacles, and maintain a resilient attitude in the pursuit of goals. In this section, we will explore how attitude intelligence influences goal setting and how it can be harnessed to achieve success in various areas of life.

The Role of Attitude in Goal Setting

Attitude plays a crucial role in goal setting as it determines our mindset and approach towards achieving our objectives. A positive attitude enables us to believe in our abilities, stay motivated, and persevere in the face of challenges. On the other hand, a negative attitude can hinder progress, create self-doubt, and lead to a lack of commitment.

When setting goals, it is important to adopt a positive attitude. This involves cultivating a belief in our own capabilities, maintaining optimism, and embracing a growth mindset. With a positive attitude, we are more likely to set ambitious and meaningful goals, as well as remain resilient and motivated throughout the journey.

Aligning Attitude with Goals

To effectively harness attitude intelligence in goal setting, it is essential to align our attitude with our goals. This means ensuring that our mindset, beliefs, and values are in harmony with the objectives we wish to achieve. When our attitude is congruent with our goals, we are more likely to stay committed, take consistent action, and overcome obstacles along the way.

One way to align attitude with goals is by setting goals that are personally meaningful and aligned with our values. When we have a strong emotional connection to our goals, we are more likely to maintain a positive attitude and stay motivated, even when faced with challenges. Additionally, it is important to regularly evaluate and adjust our attitude to ensure it remains aligned with our evolving goals and aspirations.

Developing an Attitude of Possibility

An attitude of possibility is a key component of attitude intelligence in goal setting. It involves cultivating a mindset that focuses on opportunities, growth, and solutions rather than limitations and obstacles. With an attitude of possibility, we are more likely to set ambitious goals, embrace challenges as learning opportunities, and persist in the face of setbacks.

To develop an attitude of possibility, it is important to challenge limiting beliefs and replace them with empowering ones. This can be done through self-reflection, positive affirmations, and surrounding ourselves with supportive and optimistic individuals. By consciously choosing to adopt an attitude of possibility, we open ourselves up to new possibilities and increase our chances of achieving our goals.

Overcoming Obstacles with Attitude Intelligence

Obstacles are an inevitable part of any journey towards achieving goals. However, with attitude intelligence, we can navigate through obstacles more effectively and maintain a positive mindset. Attitude intelligence allows us to view obstacles as opportunities for growth, learn from setbacks, and find alternative solutions.

When faced with obstacles, it is important to approach them with a solution-oriented mindset. This involves reframing challenges as opportunities, seeking support and guidance when needed, and maintaining a positive attitude even in the face of adversity. By leveraging attitude intelligence, we can overcome obstacles with resilience, creativity, and determination.

The Power of Visualization and Positive Affirmations

Visualization and positive affirmations are powerful tools that can enhance goal setting and attitude intelligence. Visualization involves mentally picturing ourselves achieving our goals and experiencing the associated emotions and sensations. Positive affirmations, on the other hand, are statements that reinforce positive beliefs and attitudes.

By regularly visualizing our goals and affirming positive beliefs, we can strengthen our attitude intelligence. Visualization helps to create a clear mental image of our desired outcomes, while positive affirmations reinforce empowering beliefs and attitudes. These practices not only enhance motivation and focus but also help to align our subconscious mind with our conscious goals.

Celebrating Milestones and Practicing Gratitude

In the pursuit of goals, it is important to celebrate milestones and practice gratitude along the way. Celebrating milestones allows us to acknowledge our progress, boost motivation, and maintain a positive attitude. It provides a sense of accomplishment and reinforces the belief that we are capable of achieving our goals.

Practicing gratitude involves expressing appreciation for the journey, the lessons learned, and the support received. Gratitude helps to cultivate a positive attitude by shifting our focus from what is lacking to what we already have. By regularly acknowledging and expressing gratitude, we can maintain a positive mindset and enhance our attitude intelligence.

Conclusion

Goal setting is a powerful tool for personal development and achievement. When combined with attitude intelligence, it becomes even more impactful. Attitude intelligence influences goal setting by shaping our mindset, aligning our attitude with our goals, and enabling us to overcome obstacles. By developing an attitude of possibility, leveraging visualization and positive affirmations, and practicing gratitude, we can enhance our attitude intelligence and increase our chances of achieving success in all areas of life.

5.3 Overcoming Obstacles with Attitude

Attitude Intelligence plays a crucial role in overcoming obstacles and challenges that we encounter in various aspects of life. Whether it's in our personal relationships, professional life, health and well-being, personal development, or any other area, having the right attitude can make all the difference in how we navigate and conquer the hurdles that come our way.

The Power of a Positive Attitude

A positive attitude is a key component of Attitude Intelligence when it comes to overcoming obstacles. It is the mindset that allows us to see challenges as opportunities for growth and learning, rather than as roadblocks. With a positive attitude, we approach obstacles with resilience, determination, and a belief in our ability to overcome them.

When faced with obstacles, individuals with a positive attitude tend to focus on solutions rather than dwelling on the problem itself. They maintain a sense of optimism and hope, which fuels their motivation to find creative ways to overcome the challenges they face. This positive mindset enables them to persevere through difficult times and emerge stronger on the other side.

Developing a Growth Mindset

One of the key aspects of Attitude Intelligence in overcoming obstacles is developing a growth mindset. A growth mindset is the belief that our abilities and intelligence can be developed through dedication, effort, and learning from failures. It is the understanding that setbacks and obstacles are not permanent limitations but opportunities for growth and improvement.

Individuals with a growth mindset view obstacles as stepping stones to success rather than insurmountable barriers. They embrace challenges as chances to learn, adapt, and develop new skills. This mindset allows them to approach obstacles with a sense of curiosity and a willingness to try different strategies until they find what works.

Embracing Resilience

Resilience is another crucial aspect of Attitude Intelligence when it comes to overcoming obstacles. Resilience is the ability to bounce back from setbacks, adapt to change, and maintain a positive attitude in the face of adversity. It is the inner strength that allows us to persevere and keep moving forward, even when things get tough.

Resilient individuals understand that obstacles are a natural part of life and that setbacks are temporary. They view challenges as opportunities for personal growth and development. Instead of allowing obstacles to discourage them, they use them as fuel to become stronger and more determined.

Cultivating a Problem-Solving Attitude

Attitude Intelligence also involves cultivating a problem-solving attitude when faced with obstacles. Instead of getting overwhelmed or giving up, individuals with a problem-solving attitude approach obstacles with a proactive mindset. They analyze the situation, identify potential solutions, and take action to overcome the challenge.

A problem-solving attitude involves breaking down the obstacle into smaller, manageable tasks. It requires creativity, resourcefulness, and the ability to think outside the box. Individuals with this attitude are not afraid to seek help or advice when needed, and they are open to exploring different approaches until they find a solution.

Building Resilient Support Systems

Overcoming obstacles becomes easier when we have a strong support system in place. Surrounding ourselves with positive, supportive individuals who believe in us and our abilities can significantly impact our Attitude Intelligence. These individuals can provide encouragement, guidance, and practical assistance when we face challenges.

Building a resilient support system involves nurturing relationships with people who share our values, goals, and positive attitudes. It also means being willing to offer support to others in their times of need. Together, we can face obstacles with a collective strength and a shared belief in our ability to overcome any challenge that comes our way.

Conclusion

Attitude Intelligence is a powerful tool for overcoming obstacles in every aspect of life. By cultivating a positive attitude, developing a growth mindset, embracing resilience, and adopting a problem-solving attitude, we can navigate through challenges with grace and determination. Building a strong support system further enhances our ability to overcome obstacles and emerge stronger on the other side. With Attitude Intelligence, we can face any obstacle that life throws at us and turn it into an opportunity for growth and success.

5.4 Continuous Learning and Attitude Intelligence

Continuous learning is a fundamental aspect of personal development and growth. It involves the ongoing acquisition of knowledge, skills, and experiences throughout one's life. When combined with attitude intelligence, continuous learning becomes a powerful tool for personal and professional success.

Attitude intelligence plays a crucial role in continuous learning. It is the mindset and approach we bring to the process of acquiring new knowledge and skills. With a positive and open attitude, we can embrace learning opportunities, overcome challenges, and adapt to new situations. Attitude intelligence enables us to approach learning with curiosity, enthusiasm, and a growth mindset.

The Importance of Continuous Learning

In today's rapidly changing world, continuous learning is more important than ever. The knowledge and skills we acquire early in our lives may become outdated or insufficient over time. Continuous learning allows us to stay relevant, adapt to new technologies and trends, and remain competitive in our personal and professional lives.

Moreover, continuous learning enhances our personal growth and fulfillment. It expands our horizons, broadens our perspectives, and enables us to explore new interests and passions. It fosters intellectual curiosity, creativity, and critical thinking skills. By continuously learning, we can unlock our full potential and lead more fulfilling lives.

Attitude Intelligence and Continuous Learning

Attitude intelligence is closely intertwined with continuous learning. It shapes our approach to learning and determines how effectively we can acquire and apply new knowledge and skills. Here are some ways in which attitude intelligence enhances continuous learning:

1. Embracing Challenges

Attitude intelligence enables us to embrace challenges and view them as opportunities for growth. Instead of shying away from difficult tasks or fearing failure, we approach them with a positive attitude and a willingness to learn. We understand that challenges provide valuable learning experiences and help us develop resilience and problem-solving skills.

2. Cultivating a Growth Mindset

A growth mindset is a belief that our abilities and intelligence can be developed through dedication and hard work. Attitude intelligence fosters a growth mindset, allowing us to believe in our capacity to learn and improve. With a growth mindset, we are more likely to persevere through setbacks, seek feedback, and continuously strive for improvement.

3. Seeking Feedback and Constructive Criticism

Attitude intelligence encourages us to seek feedback and constructive criticism from others. We understand that feedback is a valuable source of learning and growth. By actively seeking feedback, we can identify areas for improvement, gain new perspectives, and refine our skills. This feedback loop accelerates our learning process and helps us reach our goals more effectively.

4. Embracing Lifelong Learning

Attitude intelligence promotes the belief that learning is a lifelong journey. It encourages us to seek out new knowledge and skills, even outside of formal educational settings. We understand that learning opportunities exist in everyday experiences, interactions, and challenges. By embracing lifelong learning, we can continuously expand our knowledge, stay adaptable, and remain intellectually engaged.

5. Adapting to Change

Attitude intelligence equips us with the ability to adapt to change. In today's fast-paced world, change is inevitable. By maintaining a positive attitude and embracing change as an opportunity for growth, we can navigate through transitions more effectively. Attitude intelligence enables us to be flexible, open-minded, and willing to learn new ways of doing things.

Strategies for Developing Attitude Intelligence in Continuous Learning

Developing attitude intelligence in continuous learning requires conscious effort and practice. Here are some strategies to cultivate attitude intelligence in your learning journey:

1. Set Learning Goals

Set clear and specific learning goals that align with your interests and aspirations. Having goals provides direction and motivation for your continuous learning journey. Break down your goals into smaller, achievable milestones to track your progress and celebrate your achievements along the way.

2. Embrace a Growth Mindset

Adopt a growth mindset by believing in your ability to learn and improve. Embrace challenges, view setbacks as learning opportunities, and persist in the face of obstacles. Cultivate a positive attitude towards failure, understanding that it is an essential part of the learning process.

3. Seek Diverse Learning Experiences

Expose yourself to a variety of learning experiences to broaden your knowledge and skills. Take advantage of online courses, workshops, seminars, and conferences. Engage in self-directed learning through reading books, listening to podcasts, or watching educational videos. Seek out mentors and experts in your field to learn from their experiences and insights.

4. Reflect and Apply Learning

Regularly reflect on your learning experiences and apply what you have learned in practical situations. Reflective practice enhances understanding and retention of knowledge. Apply your learning to real-life scenarios, projects, or challenges to reinforce your understanding and develop practical skills.

5. Embrace Feedback

Seek feedback from mentors, peers, or experts in your field. Actively listen to their perspectives and suggestions for improvement. Use feedback as an opportunity to refine your skills and enhance your learning. Develop a growth-oriented mindset towards feedback, understanding that it is a valuable tool for continuous improvement.

6. Stay Curious and Open-Minded

Maintain a sense of curiosity and open-mindedness in your learning journey. Be willing to explore new ideas, challenge your existing beliefs, and consider different perspectives. Embrace the joy of learning and approach new topics with enthusiasm and a thirst for knowledge.

Continuous learning, combined with attitude intelligence, is a powerful combination for personal and professional growth. By embracing a positive attitude, seeking out learning opportunities, and cultivating a growth mindset, you can unlock your full potential and thrive in every aspect of life.

Chapter 6

Attitude Intelligence in Financial Success

6.1 Attitude and Money Mindset

Having the right attitude towards money is crucial for financial success and overall well-being. Your mindset and beliefs about money can greatly impact your financial decisions, habits, and ultimately your financial independence. In this section, we will explore the relationship between attitude and money mindset and how developing a positive attitude can lead to financial success.

The Power of Attitude in Financial Matters

Your attitude towards money plays a significant role in how you manage your finances and make financial decisions. If you have a negative attitude towards money, such as believing that it is scarce or that you will never be able to accumulate wealth, it can create a self-fulfilling prophecy. On the other hand, having a positive attitude towards money can open up opportunities and help you make wise financial choices.

Shifting to a Positive Money Mindset

Developing a positive money mindset starts with recognizing and challenging any negative beliefs or attitudes you may have about money. It's important to understand that money is a tool that can be used to create a better life for yourself and others. Here are some strategies to help you shift to a positive money mindset:

1. **Identify and challenge limiting beliefs:** Take a moment to

reflect on your beliefs about money. Are there any negative or limiting beliefs that are holding you back? Common limiting beliefs include "money is evil" or "rich people are greedy." Challenge these beliefs by seeking evidence to the contrary and replacing them with positive affirmations.

2. **Practice gratitude:** Cultivating an attitude of gratitude towards money can help shift your mindset. Instead of focusing on what you lack, appreciate what you already have. Express gratitude for the money you earn, the opportunities it provides, and the financial resources available to you.

3. **Visualize your financial goals:** Create a clear vision of your financial goals and visualize yourself achieving them. This helps to create a positive and optimistic mindset, reinforcing the belief that you can achieve financial success.

4. **Educate yourself:** Expand your financial knowledge and skills. Read books, attend seminars, or take courses on personal finance and investing. The more you understand about money, the more confident and empowered you will feel in managing your finances.

5. **Surround yourself with positive influences:** Surround yourself with people who have a positive attitude towards money and financial success. Engage in conversations about money that are empowering and supportive. Avoid negative influences that perpetuate scarcity mindset or unhealthy financial habits.

The Role of Attitude in Financial Decision Making

Your attitude towards money can significantly influence your financial decision-making process. A positive attitude can help you make rational and informed decisions, while a negative attitude can lead to impulsive or fear-based choices. Here are some ways in which attitude impacts financial decision making:

1. **Risk tolerance:** Your attitude towards risk plays a crucial role in investment decisions. A positive attitude towards risk can enable you to take calculated risks and potentially earn higher returns. Conversely, a negative attitude towards risk may lead to avoiding investments altogether, potentially limiting your financial growth.

2. **Delayed gratification:** A positive money mindset encourages delayed gratification, understanding that short-term sacrifices can lead to long-term financial success. This attitude allows you to prioritize saving and investing over immediate spending, leading to greater financial security in the future.

3. **Financial discipline:** A positive attitude towards money promotes financial discipline. It helps you develop healthy spending habits, avoid unnecessary debt, and stick to a budget. With a positive attitude, you are more likely to make conscious choices aligned with your long-term financial goals.

4. **Opportunity mindset:** Having a positive attitude towards money allows you to see opportunities where others may see obstacles. It enables you to think creatively and seek out new ways to generate income or invest wisely. This mindset opens doors to financial growth and abundance.

Cultivating a Positive Money Mindset

Cultivating a positive money mindset is an ongoing process that requires self-awareness, practice, and perseverance. Here are some additional strategies to help you develop and maintain a positive attitude towards money:

1. **Practice affirmations:** Repeat positive affirmations about money regularly. Affirmations such as "I am worthy of financial abundance" or "I attract wealth and prosperity" can help reprogram your subconscious mind and reinforce positive beliefs about money.

2. **Celebrate financial wins:** Acknowledge and celebrate your financial achievements, no matter how small. This reinforces a positive attitude towards money and motivates you to continue making progress towards your financial goals.

3. **Learn from setbacks:** View financial setbacks as learning opportunities rather than failures. Adopting a growth mindset allows you to learn from mistakes, make necessary adjustments, and move forward with a positive attitude.

4. **Give back:** Practice generosity and giving. Sharing your financial resources with others in need cultivates a mindset of abundance and gratitude. It reinforces the belief that there is always enough to go around and encourages a positive attitude towards money.

Remember, developing a positive money mindset is a journey that requires consistent effort and self-reflection. By adopting a positive attitude towards money, you can transform your financial life and create a future of abundance and financial independence.

6.2 Building Wealth with a Positive Attitude

Building wealth is a goal that many people strive for in their lives. It involves accumulating financial resources and assets that can provide security, freedom, and opportunities for oneself and one's family. While there are various strategies and techniques for building wealth, one often overlooked factor that plays a significant role in achieving financial success is attitude intelligence.

Attitude intelligence refers to the ability to cultivate and maintain a positive mindset and outlook towards wealth creation. It involves developing a set of beliefs, attitudes, and behaviors that support financial growth and abundance. A positive attitude towards wealth can have a profound impact on one's financial journey, influencing decisions, actions, and outcomes.

The Power of a Positive Attitude

A positive attitude is a key driver of success in any endeavor, including wealth building. It shapes our thoughts, emotions, and actions, ultimately influencing the results we achieve. When it comes to building wealth, a positive attitude can make a significant difference in several ways:

1. **Belief in abundance:** A positive attitude towards wealth involves believing in the abundance of opportunities and resources available. It allows individuals to see possibilities where others may see limitations, enabling them to seize opportunities and take calculated risks.

2. **Motivation and persistence:** Building wealth requires dedication, hard work, and perseverance. A positive attitude provides the motivation and resilience needed to overcome challenges and setbacks along the way. It helps individuals stay focused on their goals and maintain the determination to keep moving forward, even in the face of adversity.

3. **Optimistic mindset:** A positive attitude fosters an optimistic mindset, which is essential for making sound financial decisions. It allows individuals to approach investment opportunities with confidence and optimism, rather than fear or doubt. This mindset enables them to take calculated risks and make informed decisions that can lead to long-term financial growth.

4. **Attracting opportunities:** A positive attitude has a magnetic effect, attracting opportunities and like-minded individuals. When individuals radiate positivity and optimism, they tend to attract people and circumstances that align with their goals and aspirations. This can open doors to new business ventures, partnerships, and investment opportunities that can accelerate wealth creation.

Cultivating a Positive Attitude towards Wealth

While some individuals may naturally possess a positive attitude towards wealth, others may need to consciously cultivate it. Here are some strategies to develop and maintain a positive attitude towards building wealth:

1. **Self-awareness:** Start by becoming aware of your current attitudes and beliefs about wealth. Identify any negative or limiting beliefs that may be holding you back from achieving financial success. Challenge these beliefs and replace them with positive, empowering ones.

2. **Gratitude:** Cultivate a sense of gratitude for the resources and opportunities you currently have. Appreciating what you already have creates a positive mindset and attracts more abundance into your life. Practice gratitude daily by acknowledging and expressing thanks for the wealth and abundance in your life, no matter how small.

3. **Visualization:** Use the power of visualization to create a clear mental image of your desired financial future. Visualize yourself achieving your wealth goals, experiencing the lifestyle you desire, and enjoying financial freedom. This practice helps align your subconscious mind with your conscious goals, reinforcing a positive attitude towards wealth.

4. **Positive affirmations:** Affirmations are positive statements that reinforce desired beliefs and attitudes. Create a list of affirmations related to wealth and abundance, such as "I am worthy of financial success" or "I attract wealth and opportunities effortlessly." Repeat these affirmations daily to reprogram your subconscious mind and reinforce a positive attitude towards wealth.

5. **Surround yourself with positivity:** Surround yourself with individuals who have a positive attitude towards wealth and success. Engage in conversations, join communities, or seek

mentors who can inspire and support your financial journey. Avoid negative influences or individuals who discourage your aspirations.

6. **Continuous learning:** Invest in your financial education and personal development. The more knowledge and skills you acquire, the more confident and empowered you will feel in your wealth-building journey. Attend seminars, read books, listen to podcasts, and seek out experts in the field of finance and wealth creation.

The Impact of a Positive Attitude on Wealth Building

A positive attitude towards wealth can have a profound impact on one's financial journey. It influences the decisions individuals make, the actions they take, and the opportunities they attract. Here are some ways a positive attitude can contribute to building wealth:

1. **Risk-taking:** A positive attitude enables individuals to take calculated risks and step out of their comfort zones. It allows them to see potential rewards rather than focusing solely on potential losses. This willingness to take risks can lead to investment opportunities that have the potential for significant financial gains.

2. **Persistence:** Building wealth requires persistence and resilience. A positive attitude provides the motivation and determination to keep going, even when faced with challenges or setbacks. It helps individuals maintain focus on their long-term goals and stay committed to their wealth-building strategies.

3. **Networking and partnerships:** A positive attitude attracts like-minded individuals and opportunities for collaboration. By radiating positivity and optimism, individuals can build strong networks and form partnerships that can accelerate wealth creation. Collaborating with others who share similar

goals and values can lead to joint ventures, shared resources, and increased access to opportunities.

4. **Creativity and innovation:** A positive attitude fosters creativity and innovation, which are essential for wealth creation. It encourages individuals to think outside the box, explore new ideas, and find innovative solutions to financial challenges. This mindset can lead to the development of unique business ventures or investment strategies that set individuals apart from the competition.

5. **Long-term perspective:** A positive attitude helps individuals maintain a long-term perspective on wealth building. It allows them to focus on sustainable growth and wealth preservation rather than short-term gains. This mindset promotes wise financial decision-making and reduces the likelihood of impulsive or risky actions that could jeopardize long-term financial success.

In conclusion, building wealth with a positive attitude is not just about financial strategies and techniques; it is about cultivating a mindset that supports abundance, resilience, and growth. A positive attitude towards wealth can shape one's financial journey, influencing decisions, actions, and outcomes. By developing and maintaining a positive attitude, individuals can unlock their full potential for financial success and create a life of abundance and prosperity.

6.3 Attitude and Financial Decision Making

Financial decision making is a crucial aspect of our lives. Whether it's managing our personal finances, making investments, or planning for retirement, the choices we make can have a significant impact on our financial well-being. Attitude intelligence plays a vital role in guiding our financial decision-making process and ultimately determining our financial success.

Attitude intelligence in the context of financial decision making refers to the ability to approach financial matters with a positive and proactive mindset. It involves having the right attitude towards money, understanding the importance of financial planning, and making informed choices based on careful analysis and consideration.

One of the key aspects of attitude intelligence in financial decision making is developing a healthy money mindset. Our attitude towards money can greatly influence our financial decisions. If we have a negative mindset, filled with fear, scarcity, and a lack of confidence, it can hinder our ability to make sound financial choices. On the other hand, a positive and abundance mindset can empower us to make wise decisions, take calculated risks, and seize opportunities for financial growth.

Having a positive attitude towards money means viewing it as a tool for achieving our goals and creating a better life, rather than seeing it as a source of stress or a measure of our self-worth. It involves cultivating a mindset of abundance, believing that there are always opportunities to earn, save, and invest wisely.

Attitude intelligence also involves understanding the importance of financial planning and setting clear financial goals. Without a plan, our financial decisions may lack direction and purpose. By setting specific, measurable, achievable, relevant, and time-bound (SMART) goals, we can align our financial decisions with our long-term aspirations.

When making financial decisions, it is essential to gather relevant information and analyze the potential risks and rewards. Attitude intelligence encourages us to approach financial decision making with a rational and objective mindset. It involves conducting thorough research, seeking advice from experts, and considering various options before making a choice.

Another crucial aspect of attitude intelligence in financial decision making is the ability to manage emotions effectively. Emotions such as fear, greed, and impatience can cloud our judgment and lead to impulsive and irrational financial decisions. Attitude intelligence helps us recognize and regulate these emotions, allowing us to make decisions based on logic and reason rather than being driven by short-term impulses.

Furthermore, attitude intelligence encourages us to take a long-term perspective when making financial decisions. It reminds us that financial success is not achieved overnight but requires patience, discipline, and perseverance. By focusing on long-term goals and avoiding short-term temptations, we can make decisions that align with our overall financial well-being.

Attitude intelligence also emphasizes the importance of learning from our financial mistakes and failures. Instead of dwelling on past failures, it encourages us to view them as valuable learning experiences. By adopting a growth mindset, we can use these experiences to improve our financial decision-making skills and make better choices in the future.

In addition to individual financial decision making, attitude intelligence also extends to collaborative financial decisions in partnerships or marriages. It involves effective communication, mutual respect, and shared financial goals. By approaching financial decisions with a positive attitude and open-mindedness, couples can work together to achieve financial harmony and build a secure future.

In conclusion, attitude intelligence plays a significant role in financial decision making. It involves developing a positive money mindset, setting clear financial goals, gathering relevant information, managing emotions effectively, taking a long-term perspective, and learning from past mistakes. By cultivating attitude intelligence, we can make informed and empowered financial decisions that lead to financial success and overall well-being.

6.4 Attitude Intelligence for Financial Independence

Attitude Intelligence plays a crucial role in achieving financial independence. It is not just about having a positive mindset towards money; it involves developing a comprehensive understanding of financial principles, making informed decisions, and taking proactive steps towards financial goals. In this section, we will explore how Attitude Intelligence can empower individuals to attain financial independence and create a secure future.

The Power of Attitude in Financial Success

Attitude plays a significant role in determining our financial success. A positive attitude towards money can help us develop healthy financial habits, such as budgeting, saving, and investing. It enables us to view money as a tool for achieving our goals rather than a source of stress or anxiety.

Attitude Intelligence helps us cultivate a growth mindset towards finances. Instead of being limited by our current financial situation, we believe in our ability to improve and grow our wealth. This mindset encourages us to seek opportunities, take calculated risks, and learn from our financial experiences.

Developing a Wealth Mindset

Attitude Intelligence involves developing a wealth mindset, which is essential for achieving financial independence. A wealth mindset is characterized by a belief in abundance, a focus on long-term goals, and a willingness to take calculated risks.

To develop a wealth mindset, it is crucial to challenge any limiting beliefs or negative attitudes towards money. We need to shift our perspective from scarcity to abundance and believe that there are ample opportunities to create wealth. This mindset allows us to approach financial decisions with confidence and optimism.

Building Financial Literacy

Attitude Intelligence goes hand in hand with financial literacy. It is essential to educate ourselves about financial concepts, such as budgeting, investing, and debt management. By acquiring knowledge and understanding financial principles, we can make informed decisions and take control of our financial future.

Financial literacy empowers us to develop a strategic approach towards money. We can create a budget that aligns with our goals, track our expenses, and make conscious spending choices. Moreover, understanding investment options and strategies enables us to grow our wealth and make our money work for us.

Setting Financial Goals

Attitude Intelligence helps us set clear and achievable financial goals. By defining our objectives, we can create a roadmap towards financial independence. Setting specific, measurable, attainable, relevant, and time-bound (SMART) goals allows us to stay focused and motivated.

When setting financial goals, it is essential to consider both short-term and long-term objectives. Short-term goals may include building an emergency fund or paying off debt, while long-term goals may involve saving for retirement or purchasing a home. Attitude Intelligence helps us maintain a positive attitude throughout the journey, even when faced with challenges or setbacks.

Embracing Financial Discipline

Attitude Intelligence emphasizes the importance of financial discipline. It requires us to develop self-control and make conscious decisions that align with our financial goals. This discipline involves avoiding impulsive purchases, sticking to a budget, and prioritizing saving and investing.

Financial discipline also involves being mindful of our financial habits and behaviors. By regularly reviewing our financial situation and tracking our progress, we can identify areas for improvement and make necessary adjustments. Attitude Intelligence helps us stay committed to our financial goals and make choices that contribute to our long-term financial well-being.

Overcoming Financial Obstacles

Attitude Intelligence equips us with the resilience and determination to overcome financial obstacles. It acknowledges that setbacks and challenges are a part of the financial journey but encourages us to view them as opportunities for growth and learning.

When faced with financial difficulties, Attitude Intelligence helps us maintain a positive attitude and seek solutions. It encourages us to be proactive in finding ways to increase our income, reduce expenses, or seek professional advice when needed. By approaching obstacles with a solution-oriented mindset, we can navigate through financial challenges and continue moving towards financial independence.

Cultivating a Wealthy Lifestyle

Attitude Intelligence encourages us to cultivate a wealthy lifestyle beyond just accumulating wealth. It emphasizes the importance of financial well-being, which includes not only financial security but also a sense of fulfillment and contentment.

A wealthy lifestyle involves aligning our financial decisions with our values and priorities. It means making choices that contribute to our overall well-being, such as investing in experiences, giving back to the community, and prioritizing personal growth. Attitude Intelligence helps us find a balance between enjoying the present and planning for the future, ensuring that our financial journey is fulfilling and meaningful.

In conclusion, Attitude Intelligence plays a vital role in achieving financial independence. It involves developing a positive mindset, cultivating a wealth mindset, building financial literacy, setting clear goals, embracing financial discipline, overcoming obstacles, and cultivating a wealthy lifestyle. By harnessing the power of Attitude Intelligence, individuals can take control of their financial future, create wealth, and enjoy a life of financial independence and security.

Chapter 7

Attitude Intelligence in Education

7.1 Attitude and Learning

Attitude plays a crucial role in the process of learning. It influences how we approach new information, engage with educational activities, and ultimately, how successful we are in acquiring knowledge and skills. In this section, we will explore the connection between attitude and learning, and how developing attitude intelligence can enhance our educational experiences.

The Impact of Attitude on Learning

Our attitude towards learning greatly affects our motivation, engagement, and overall performance in educational settings. A positive attitude towards learning creates a conducive environment for growth and development. It fosters curiosity, enthusiasm, and a willingness to explore new ideas and concepts. On the other hand, a negative attitude can hinder our ability to absorb information, retain knowledge, and apply it effectively.

The Role of Attitude Intelligence in Learning

Attitude intelligence involves being aware of our attitudes towards learning and actively cultivating a positive mindset that supports our educational goals. It encompasses self-awareness, self-regulation, and the ability to adapt and respond constructively to challenges and setbacks. By developing attitude intelligence, we can optimize our learning experiences and unlock our full potential.

Cultivating a Positive Attitude towards Learning

1. **Embrace a Growth Mindset**: Adopting a growth mindset is essential for developing a positive attitude towards learning. Embrace the belief that intelligence and abilities can be developed through effort, practice, and perseverance. Emphasize the process of learning rather than focusing solely on outcomes or grades.

2. **Set Realistic Goals**: Setting realistic and achievable goals helps maintain motivation and provides a sense of direction. Break down larger goals into smaller, manageable tasks, and celebrate each milestone achieved. This approach fosters a sense of accomplishment and encourages continued progress.

3. **Find Personal Relevance**: Connect the subject matter to your own interests, passions, and goals. Understanding how the knowledge or skills being acquired can be applied in real-life situations enhances motivation and engagement. Seek out practical examples and relate the material to your own experiences.

4. **Develop Effective Study Habits**: Establishing effective study habits is crucial for optimizing learning. Create a conducive environment, manage your time efficiently, and employ active learning strategies such as summarizing, questioning, and self-testing. Regular review and practice reinforce understanding and retention.

5. **Seek Support and Collaboration**: Don't hesitate to seek support from teachers, mentors, or peers when facing challenges or needing clarification. Collaborating with others can provide different perspectives, enhance understanding, and foster a sense of community and shared learning.

6. **Maintain a Positive Mindset**: Cultivate a positive attitude towards challenges and setbacks. View them as opportunities for growth and learning rather than insurmountable obstacles. Practice self-compassion and embrace a mindset of

continuous improvement.

Overcoming Learning Barriers with Attitude Intelligence

Attitude intelligence equips us with the tools to overcome common learning barriers and maximize our educational experiences. Here are some strategies to help navigate challenges:

1. **Fear of Failure**: Fear of failure can hinder learning by creating anxiety and avoidance. Embrace a growth mindset and reframe failure as a stepping stone towards improvement. Emphasize the learning process rather than focusing solely on outcomes.

2. **Lack of Motivation**: When faced with a lack of motivation, revisit your goals and find ways to make the learning experience more engaging and meaningful. Connect the material to real-life applications, seek out inspiring role models, or explore alternative learning methods.

3. **Procrastination**: Procrastination can impede learning progress. Break tasks into smaller, manageable chunks, set deadlines, and create a structured study schedule. Use techniques such as the Pomodoro Technique (working in focused bursts with short breaks) to enhance productivity.

4. **Negative Self-Talk**: Negative self-talk can undermine confidence and hinder learning. Practice positive affirmations, challenge negative thoughts, and focus on your strengths and past successes. Surround yourself with supportive and encouraging individuals.

The Benefits of Attitude Intelligence in Learning

Developing attitude intelligence in the context of learning offers numerous benefits:

1. **Enhanced Motivation**: A positive attitude towards learning

fuels intrinsic motivation, making the process enjoyable and rewarding. It increases curiosity, enthusiasm, and a desire for continuous growth.

2. **Improved Performance**: A positive attitude fosters a growth mindset, enabling individuals to embrace challenges, persist in the face of setbacks, and ultimately achieve higher levels of performance.

3. **Effective Problem-Solving**: Attitude intelligence enhances problem-solving skills by promoting a flexible and open-minded approach. It encourages individuals to think creatively, consider alternative perspectives, and explore innovative solutions.

4. **Increased Resilience**: Developing attitude intelligence equips individuals with the resilience to bounce back from failures and setbacks. It fosters a mindset that views challenges as opportunities for growth and learning.

5. **Lifelong Learning**: Attitude intelligence nurtures a love for learning and a commitment to lifelong education. It encourages individuals to seek out new knowledge, skills, and experiences beyond formal educational settings.

In conclusion, attitude intelligence plays a vital role in learning. By cultivating a positive attitude, embracing a growth mindset, and developing effective learning strategies, individuals can optimize their educational experiences, overcome barriers, and unlock their full potential. Attitude intelligence empowers individuals to approach learning with enthusiasm, curiosity, and a commitment to continuous growth.

7.2 Motivation and Attitude Intelligence

Motivation plays a crucial role in our lives, driving us to take action and pursue our goals. It is the internal force that pushes us to achieve, overcome obstacles, and strive for success. However, motivation alone is not enough to guarantee sustained progress and fulfillment. Attitude intelligence, the ability to cultivate and maintain a positive attitude, is equally important in harnessing motivation and maximizing its potential.

Attitude intelligence and motivation are closely intertwined. While motivation provides the initial spark, attitude intelligence fuels the fire and keeps it burning. It is the mindset and perspective we adopt that determine how we interpret and respond to challenges, setbacks, and opportunities. With a positive attitude, we are more likely to stay motivated, persevere in the face of adversity, and maintain a sense of purpose and enthusiasm.

One of the key aspects of attitude intelligence in relation to motivation is self-belief. When we have a positive attitude towards ourselves and our abilities, we are more likely to believe in our potential to succeed. This self-belief acts as a powerful motivator, driving us to set ambitious goals and work towards achieving them. On the other hand, a negative attitude can undermine our motivation by eroding our confidence and creating self-doubt.

Attitude intelligence also influences our perception of challenges. With a positive attitude, we view challenges as opportunities for growth and learning. We see them as stepping stones towards our goals rather than insurmountable obstacles. This mindset shift not only enhances our motivation but also increases our resilience in the face of setbacks. We are more likely to persist and find creative solutions when we approach challenges with a positive attitude.

Furthermore, attitude intelligence helps us maintain motivation during difficult times. Life is full of ups and downs, and there will inevitably be moments when our motivation wanes. However, with a positive attitude, we can weather these storms and find the strength to keep going. A positive attitude allows us to reframe setbacks as temporary and see them as opportunities for growth. It helps us maintain a long-term perspective and stay focused on our goals, even when the going gets tough.

In addition to self-motivation, attitude intelligence also influences our ability to motivate and inspire others. Our attitude and energy are contagious, and they have a profound impact on those around us. When we approach tasks and challenges with enthusiasm and optimism, we inspire others to do the same. Our positive attitude can create a ripple effect, fostering a supportive and motivated environment where everyone can thrive.

To cultivate attitude intelligence and enhance motivation, there are several strategies we can employ:

1. Self-reflection: Take time to reflect on your attitude and mindset. Identify any negative thought patterns or limiting beliefs that may be hindering your motivation. Challenge these beliefs and replace them with positive and empowering thoughts.

2. Goal setting: Set clear and meaningful goals that align with your values and aspirations. Break them down into smaller, achievable steps to maintain motivation and track progress. Celebrate milestones along the way to stay motivated and reinforce a positive attitude.

3. Surround yourself with positivity: Surround yourself with positive influences, whether it be supportive friends and family or motivational books and podcasts. Engage in activities that uplift and inspire you, and minimize exposure

to negativity and toxic environments.

4. Practice gratitude: Cultivate a mindset of gratitude by regularly acknowledging and appreciating the blessings in your life. Gratitude helps shift your focus towards the positive aspects of your journey, enhancing motivation and fostering a positive attitude.

5. Embrace failure as a learning opportunity: Adopt a growth mindset and view failure as a stepping stone towards success. Learn from your mistakes, adjust your approach, and keep moving forward. A positive attitude towards failure fuels motivation and encourages resilience.

6. Take care of your well-being: Physical and mental well-being are essential for maintaining motivation and a positive attitude. Prioritize self-care activities such as exercise, healthy eating, and sufficient rest. Engage in practices like mindfulness and meditation to cultivate a calm and focused mindset.

By integrating these strategies into our lives, we can enhance our attitude intelligence and leverage motivation to achieve our goals. Attitude intelligence is a powerful tool that empowers us to navigate the challenges of life with resilience, optimism, and unwavering motivation. It is the key to unlocking our full potential and living a fulfilling and purpose-driven life.

7.3 Attitude and Academic Success

Attitude plays a crucial role in determining academic success. It is not just about intelligence or knowledge; having the right attitude towards learning and education can significantly impact a student's performance and overall achievements. In this section, we will explore the connection between attitude and academic success and discuss how attitude intelligence can be developed to enhance educational outcomes.

The Power of a Positive Attitude

A positive attitude is essential for academic success. When students approach their studies with a positive mindset, they are more likely to be motivated, engaged, and resilient in the face of challenges. A positive attitude fosters a growth mindset, which is the belief that abilities and intelligence can be developed through effort and perseverance.

Students with a positive attitude are more likely to set realistic goals, work diligently towards them, and maintain a sense of optimism even when faced with setbacks. They view failures as opportunities for growth and are willing to put in the necessary effort to improve. This mindset not only enhances academic performance but also promotes a love for learning and a lifelong pursuit of knowledge.

Attitude and Learning

Attitude influences how students approach the learning process. Those with a positive attitude are more likely to be actively engaged in their studies, seeking out opportunities to expand their knowledge and understanding. They approach learning with curiosity and enthusiasm, making connections between different concepts and applying their knowledge to real-world situations.

On the other hand, students with a negative attitude may view learning as a chore or a means to an end. They may lack motivation and struggle to find relevance in what they are studying. This negative mindset can hinder their ability to grasp new concepts, retain information, and perform well academically.

Motivation and Attitude Intelligence

Motivation is a key component of academic success, and attitude plays a significant role in driving and sustaining motivation. Students with a positive attitude are intrinsically motivated, meaning they are driven by their own internal desires and interests rather than external rewards or pressures. They have a genuine passion for learning and derive satisfaction from the process itself, not just the end result.

Attitude intelligence helps students develop and maintain motivation by cultivating a growth mindset and setting meaningful goals. By believing in their ability to improve and achieve, students are more likely to stay motivated even when faced with challenges or setbacks. They understand that effort and perseverance are essential for success and are willing to put in the necessary work to reach their goals.

Attitude and Academic Performance

Numerous studies have shown a strong correlation between attitude and academic performance. Students with a positive attitude tend to achieve higher grades, perform better on tests, and demonstrate a deeper understanding of the subject matter. Their positive mindset allows them to approach exams and assignments with confidence, leading to improved performance.

Additionally, a positive attitude can enhance critical thinking skills, problem-solving abilities, and creativity. Students who believe in their own capabilities are more likely to take risks, think outside the box, and explore different perspectives. This mindset fosters a deeper level of engagement with the material and promotes a more comprehensive understanding of the subject.

Developing Attitude Intelligence for Academic Success

Developing attitude intelligence is a lifelong process, and it requires conscious effort and self-reflection. Here are some strategies to cultivate a positive attitude and enhance academic success:

1. **Self-awareness**: Reflect on your current attitude towards learning and identify any negative beliefs or thought patterns that may be holding you back. Challenge these beliefs and replace them with positive affirmations and a growth mindset.

2. **Goal setting**: Set realistic and meaningful goals that align with your interests and aspirations. Break down larger goals into smaller, manageable tasks, and celebrate your achievements along the way. This will help maintain

motivation and provide a sense of accomplishment.

3. **Time management**: Develop effective time management skills to prioritize your studies and allocate dedicated time for learning. Create a study schedule that allows for regular breaks and ensures a healthy work-life balance.

4. **Seek support**: Surround yourself with positive influences, such as supportive friends, mentors, or teachers who can provide guidance and encouragement. Collaborate with classmates and engage in group study sessions to foster a sense of community and shared learning.

5. **Embrace challenges**: View challenges as opportunities for growth and learning. Embrace the process of overcoming obstacles and celebrate the lessons learned along the way. Develop resilience and perseverance in the face of setbacks.

6. **Practice self-care**: Take care of your physical and mental well-being by getting enough sleep, eating nutritious meals, and engaging in regular exercise. Prioritize self-care activities that help reduce stress and promote overall well-being.

By developing attitude intelligence and cultivating a positive attitude towards learning, students can unlock their full potential and achieve academic success. Remember, attitude is not something fixed or predetermined; it can be shaped and developed through conscious effort and a commitment to personal growth.

7.4 Developing a Growth Mindset with Attitude Intelligence

In our journey of developing attitude intelligence, one crucial aspect that deserves special attention is the cultivation of a growth mindset. A growth mindset is the belief that our abilities and intelligence can be developed through dedication, effort, and a willingness to learn. It is the understanding that our potential is not fixed, but rather malleable, and that we can continuously improve and grow.

When we combine the power of a growth mindset with attitude intelligence, we unlock a powerful tool for personal and professional development. Developing a growth mindset with attitude intelligence allows us to approach challenges, setbacks, and opportunities with a positive and proactive attitude. It enables us to embrace learning, adapt to change, and persevere in the face of obstacles.

The Power of a Growth Mindset

A growth mindset is rooted in the belief that our abilities are not predetermined, but rather can be developed through effort and learning. This mindset empowers us to view failures and setbacks as opportunities for growth and improvement. Instead of being discouraged by challenges, individuals with a growth mindset see them as stepping stones towards success.

With a growth mindset, we understand that our intelligence, talents, and skills can be enhanced through dedication and hard work. This belief fosters a love for learning and a desire to continuously improve. It allows us to embrace feedback and criticism as valuable tools for growth, rather than taking them personally or becoming defensive.

Attitude Intelligence and the Growth Mindset

Attitude intelligence complements the growth mindset by providing the framework and strategies to cultivate a positive and proactive attitude towards learning and personal development. It helps us harness the power of our mindset and channel it towards achieving our goals.

One of the key aspects of attitude intelligence in developing a growth mindset is self-awareness. By being aware of our thoughts, beliefs, and attitudes towards learning and growth, we can identify any limiting beliefs or negative self-talk that may hinder our progress. Attitude intelligence empowers us to challenge and reframe these limiting beliefs, replacing them with positive and empowering thoughts.

Attitude intelligence also emphasizes the importance of perseverance and resilience. Developing a growth mindset requires us to embrace challenges and setbacks as opportunities for growth. It requires us to persist in the face of obstacles and setbacks, knowing that they are an essential part of the learning process. Attitude intelligence equips us with the tools to maintain a positive attitude and bounce back from failures, setbacks, and disappointments.

Strategies for Developing a Growth Mindset with Attitude Intelligence

To develop a growth mindset with attitude intelligence, we can implement several strategies and practices into our daily lives:

1. Embrace challenges: Instead of avoiding challenges, actively seek them out. View them as opportunities to learn and grow, and approach them with a positive and open mindset.

2. Cultivate a love for learning: Develop a curiosity and thirst for knowledge. Embrace new experiences, explore different perspectives, and continuously seek opportunities for personal and professional development.

3. Embrace failure as a learning opportunity: Instead of fearing failure, see it as a stepping stone towards success. Learn from your mistakes, analyze what went wrong, and use that knowledge to improve and grow.

4. Practice self-reflection: Regularly reflect on your thoughts, beliefs, and attitudes towards learning and growth. Identify any negative or limiting beliefs and challenge them. Replace them with positive and empowering thoughts.

5. Surround yourself with positive influences: Surround yourself with individuals who have a growth mindset and a positive attitude towards learning and personal development. Their energy and mindset will inspire and motivate you to cultivate your own growth mindset.

6. Set realistic goals: Set goals that challenge you and push you out of your comfort zone. Break them down into smaller, achievable steps, and celebrate your progress along the way. This will help you stay motivated and focused on your growth journey.

7. Practice self-care: Take care of your physical, mental, and emotional well-being. A healthy body and mind are essential for maintaining a positive attitude and embracing growth.

By combining the principles of attitude intelligence with the power of a growth mindset, we can unlock our full potential and achieve remarkable personal and professional growth. Developing a growth mindset with attitude intelligence allows us to approach life with optimism, resilience, and a hunger for continuous improvement. It empowers us to embrace challenges, learn from failures, and ultimately, lead a fulfilling and successful life.

Chapter 8

Attitude Intelligence in Parenting

8.1 Attitude and Parent-Child Relationships

Parenting is one of the most important and challenging roles in life. As parents, our attitudes play a crucial role in shaping the dynamics of our relationships with our children. Attitude intelligence in parenting refers to the ability to cultivate a positive and nurturing attitude that fosters healthy parent-child relationships. It involves understanding the impact of our attitudes on our children's development and using that knowledge to create a supportive and loving environment.

The Power of Attitude in Parenting

Our attitudes as parents have a profound influence on our children's emotional well-being, behavior, and overall development. Children are highly perceptive and sensitive to their parents' attitudes and emotions. They look to us as role models and absorb our attitudes like sponges. Therefore, it is essential to cultivate a positive attitude that promotes a healthy parent-child relationship.

A positive attitude in parenting involves being loving, supportive, and empathetic towards our children. It means approaching parenting with a mindset of patience, understanding, and open communication. When we maintain a positive attitude, we create an environment where our children feel safe, valued, and encouraged to express themselves.

Building Trust and Connection

Attitude intelligence in parenting is about building trust and connection with our children. Trust is the foundation of any healthy relationship, and it is crucial in the parent-child dynamic. When we approach parenting with a positive attitude, we establish trust by consistently showing our children that we are there for them, that we listen to them, and that we respect their feelings and opinions.

A positive attitude also helps us to connect with our children on a deeper level. It allows us to understand their needs, desires, and fears. By maintaining a positive attitude, we create an environment where our children feel comfortable sharing their thoughts and emotions with us. This open communication fosters a strong bond and helps us guide them through life's challenges.

Modeling Positive Behavior

Children learn by observing and imitating their parents' behavior. Our attitudes and actions serve as powerful models for our children's behavior. When we demonstrate a positive attitude, we teach our children valuable life skills such as resilience, optimism, and problem-solving.

By modeling positive behavior, we show our children how to handle difficult situations with grace and optimism. We teach them the importance of perseverance and the value of a positive mindset. When our children see us approaching challenges with a positive attitude, they are more likely to adopt the same approach in their own lives.

Effective Communication

Attitude intelligence in parenting also involves effective communication. Our attitudes significantly impact the way we communicate with our children. When we maintain a positive attitude, we are more likely to communicate with empathy, patience, and understanding.

Positive communication involves active listening, validating our children's feelings, and responding with kindness and respect. It means avoiding negative language, criticism, and judgment. By communicating positively, we create an environment where our children feel heard, understood, and valued. This strengthens the parent-child relationship and fosters healthy emotional development.

Discipline with a Positive Attitude

Discipline is an essential aspect of parenting, and attitude intelligence plays a crucial role in effective discipline. Discipline with a positive attitude involves setting clear boundaries, providing consistent guidance, and using discipline as a teaching tool rather than a punishment.

When we discipline with a positive attitude, we focus on teaching our children right from wrong, rather than simply punishing them for their mistakes. We approach discipline with empathy and understanding, helping our children learn from their actions and make better choices in the future. By disciplining with a positive attitude, we create an environment where our children feel supported and encouraged to grow and learn.

Nurturing Emotional Intelligence

Emotional intelligence is the ability to recognize, understand, and manage our own emotions and the emotions of others. Attitude intelligence in parenting involves nurturing our children's emotional intelligence by modeling and teaching them how to navigate their emotions effectively.

When we maintain a positive attitude, we create a safe space for our children to express their emotions without fear of judgment or rejection. We help them develop emotional resilience by validating their feelings and teaching them healthy coping mechanisms. By nurturing their emotional intelligence, we equip our children with essential skills that will benefit them throughout their lives.

In conclusion, attitude intelligence in parenting is about cultivating a positive and nurturing attitude that fosters healthy parent-child relationships. It involves building trust, modeling positive behavior, effective communication, discipline with a positive attitude, and nurturing emotional intelligence. By developing attitude intelligence in parenting, we create an environment where our children can thrive emotionally, socially, and academically.

8.2 Positive Discipline and Attitude Intelligence

Positive discipline is an essential aspect of parenting that focuses on teaching children self-control, responsibility, and respect. It involves setting clear boundaries, providing consistent consequences, and promoting healthy communication within the parent-child relationship. When combined with attitude intelligence, positive discipline becomes a powerful tool for nurturing a child's emotional well-being and fostering their positive attitude.

The Role of Attitude Intelligence in Positive Discipline

Attitude intelligence plays a crucial role in positive discipline as it helps parents approach discipline with a positive mindset and empathetic attitude. It involves understanding the impact of our words and actions on children and recognizing that discipline is not about punishment but about teaching and guiding them towards responsible behavior.

When parents possess attitude intelligence, they are more likely to approach discipline situations with patience, understanding, and empathy. They are able to maintain a positive attitude even in challenging moments, which allows them to respond to their child's behavior in a constructive and supportive manner.

The Principles of Positive Discipline

Positive discipline is based on several key principles that align with the principles of attitude intelligence. These principles include:

1. **Mutual Respect**: Positive discipline emphasizes treating

children with respect and dignity. It involves listening to their thoughts and feelings, valuing their opinions, and involving them in decision-making processes whenever appropriate. This principle aligns with attitude intelligence's focus on fostering positive relationships and promoting empathy.

2. **Clear Boundaries**: Positive discipline involves setting clear and age-appropriate boundaries for children. These boundaries provide a sense of security and help children understand what is expected of them. Attitude intelligence recognizes the importance of clarity and consistency in communication, which is essential when establishing boundaries.

3. **Consistency**: Positive discipline requires consistency in enforcing rules and consequences. When parents consistently follow through with consequences, children learn that their actions have predictable outcomes. This consistency aligns with attitude intelligence's emphasis on being consistent in our thoughts, words, and actions.

4. **Teaching and Guidance**: Positive discipline focuses on teaching children appropriate behavior and problem-solving skills rather than simply punishing them for their mistakes. It encourages parents to explain the reasons behind rules and consequences, helping children understand the impact of their actions. Attitude intelligence recognizes the importance of teaching and guiding others towards positive attitudes and behaviors.

5. **Positive Reinforcement**: Positive discipline emphasizes the use of positive reinforcement to encourage desired behavior. Praising and acknowledging children's efforts and achievements helps build their self-esteem and motivates them to continue making positive choices. Attitude intelligence recognizes the power of positive reinforcement in

shaping attitudes and behaviors.

Applying Attitude Intelligence in Positive Discipline
To effectively apply attitude intelligence in positive discipline, parents can consider the following strategies:

1. **Self-Reflection**: Parents should regularly reflect on their own attitudes and emotions to ensure they are approaching discipline situations with a positive mindset. This self-awareness allows them to model positive behavior and respond to their child's actions in a calm and constructive manner.

2. **Empathy and Understanding**: Attitude intelligence encourages parents to empathize with their child's perspective and understand the underlying reasons for their behavior. By putting themselves in their child's shoes, parents can respond with empathy and address the root causes of misbehavior rather than focusing solely on the behavior itself.

3. **Effective Communication**: Attitude intelligence emphasizes the importance of effective communication in building positive relationships. Parents should strive to communicate clearly and respectfully with their child, using age-appropriate language and active listening skills. This open and honest communication helps children feel heard and understood.

4. **Natural Consequences**: Positive discipline encourages the use of natural consequences whenever possible. Instead of imposing arbitrary punishments, parents can allow children to experience the natural consequences of their actions, which helps them learn from their mistakes and develop problem-solving skills.

5. **Teaching Responsibility**: Attitude intelligence promotes teaching children responsibility for their actions. Parents can involve their child in problem-solving discussions, allowing

them to take ownership of their behavior and find solutions to rectify any harm caused.

6. **Positive Reinforcement**: Parents should actively look for opportunities to praise and reinforce their child's positive behavior. By focusing on the positive, parents can motivate their child to continue making responsible choices and develop a positive attitude towards themselves and others.

The Benefits of Positive Discipline and Attitude Intelligence

When positive discipline is combined with attitude intelligence, it creates a nurturing and supportive environment for children to develop a positive attitude. Some of the benefits include:

1. **Stronger Parent-Child Relationship**: Positive discipline and attitude intelligence foster a strong bond between parents and children based on trust, respect, and open communication.

2. **Emotional Well-being**: Children raised with positive discipline and attitude intelligence are more likely to have higher self-esteem, emotional resilience, and a positive outlook on life.

3. **Improved Behavior**: By focusing on teaching and guiding rather than punishing, positive discipline and attitude intelligence help children develop self-control, responsibility, and empathy towards others.

4. **Conflict Resolution Skills**: Children learn effective conflict resolution skills through positive discipline, which helps them navigate challenging situations and maintain positive relationships throughout their lives.

5. **Positive Attitude Development**: Positive discipline and attitude intelligence work hand in hand to cultivate a positive attitude in children. They learn to approach challenges with optimism, embrace growth, and develop a mindset that promotes personal and social well-being.

By incorporating positive discipline techniques and attitude intelligence into their parenting approach, parents can create a nurturing environment that supports their child's emotional growth, fosters positive attitudes, and prepares them for a successful and fulfilling life.

8.3 Teaching Resilience and Attitude

Teaching resilience and attitude is crucial in helping individuals navigate the challenges and setbacks they may encounter in life. Resilience is the ability to bounce back from adversity, while attitude plays a significant role in shaping one's response to difficult situations. By instilling resilience and a positive attitude in children, parents and educators can equip them with the necessary tools to overcome obstacles and thrive in various aspects of life.

The Importance of Teaching Resilience

Resilience is a valuable life skill that enables individuals to adapt, persevere, and grow in the face of adversity. It is essential to teach children resilience from an early age as it prepares them to handle setbacks, disappointments, and failures that they will inevitably encounter throughout their lives. By teaching resilience, we empower children to develop a mindset that views challenges as opportunities for growth rather than insurmountable obstacles.

Building Resilience through Attitude Intelligence

Attitude intelligence plays a vital role in building resilience. It involves cultivating a positive mindset, developing emotional intelligence, and fostering a sense of self-belief. By teaching children to approach challenges with a positive attitude, they learn to view setbacks as temporary and solvable. Here are some strategies to teach resilience and attitude:

1. Encourage a Growth Mindset

Teach children that their abilities and intelligence can be developed through effort and perseverance. Emphasize the importance of embracing challenges, learning from failures, and persisting in the face of obstacles. By fostering a growth mindset, children understand that their abilities are not fixed, and they have the power

8.4 Nurturing a Positive Attitude in Children

Nurturing a positive attitude in children is crucial for their overall development and well-being. A positive attitude not only helps children navigate through life's challenges but also sets the foundation for their future success and happiness. As parents and caregivers, it is our responsibility to create an environment that fosters positivity and helps children develop a resilient and optimistic mindset. In this section, we will explore various strategies and techniques to nurture a positive attitude in children.

The Power of Role Modeling

Children learn by observing and imitating the behavior of the adults around them. As parents, we have a significant influence on our children's attitudes and outlook on life. Therefore, it is essential to be mindful of our own attitudes and behaviors. By modeling a positive attitude, we can inspire and encourage our children to adopt the same mindset. Here are some ways to effectively role model a positive attitude:

1. **Maintain a positive outlook:** Show optimism and resilience in the face of challenges. Let your children see that setbacks are temporary and can be overcome with a positive attitude.

2. **Practice gratitude:** Express gratitude for the little things in life and encourage your children to do the same. This helps them develop a positive perspective and appreciate the good things around them.

3. **Manage stress effectively:** Demonstrate healthy coping mechanisms when dealing with stress. Teach your children

techniques such as deep breathing, mindfulness, and positive self-talk to manage their emotions and maintain a positive attitude.

4. **Promote kindness and empathy:** Encourage acts of kindness and teach your children to empathize with others. By fostering a sense of compassion, you help them develop a positive attitude towards others and the world.

Encouraging a Growth Mindset

A growth mindset is the belief that abilities and intelligence can be developed through effort and perseverance. Nurturing a growth mindset in children is essential for building a positive attitude towards learning and personal development. Here are some strategies to encourage a growth mindset in children:

1. **Praise effort and progress:** Instead of solely focusing on achievements, praise your children's efforts and progress. This helps them understand that hard work and perseverance are more important than immediate success.

2. **Teach the power of "yet":** Encourage your children to use the word "yet" when faced with challenges. For example, instead of saying "I can't do it," they can say "I can't do it yet." This simple shift in language promotes a belief in their ability to improve and grow.

3. **Emphasize the learning process:** Help your children understand that mistakes and failures are opportunities for growth and learning. Encourage them to reflect on their experiences, identify lessons learned, and develop strategies for improvement.

4. **Set realistic goals:** Guide your children in setting realistic and achievable goals. Break down larger goals into smaller, manageable steps, and celebrate their progress along the way. This helps them develop a positive attitude towards goal

setting and perseverance.

Creating a Positive Environment

The environment in which children grow and learn plays a significant role in shaping their attitudes. Creating a positive and nurturing environment at home and in other settings can greatly influence children's attitudes and overall well-being. Here are some ways to create a positive environment for children:

1. **Establish clear expectations:** Set clear and age-appropriate expectations for behavior and attitude. Communicate these expectations effectively and provide guidance and support to help children meet them.

2. **Encourage open communication:** Create an environment where children feel comfortable expressing their thoughts and emotions. Listen actively, validate their feelings, and provide guidance and support when needed.

3. **Celebrate achievements:** Acknowledge and celebrate your children's achievements, no matter how small. This helps build their self-confidence and reinforces a positive attitude towards their abilities.

4. **Foster a love for learning:** Encourage curiosity and a love for learning by providing opportunities for exploration and discovery. Engage in activities that stimulate their interests and encourage them to pursue their passions.

Teaching Emotional Intelligence

Emotional intelligence is the ability to recognize, understand, and manage one's own emotions and the emotions of others. By teaching children emotional intelligence, we equip them with the skills to navigate their emotions and develop a positive attitude towards themselves and others. Here are some strategies to teach emotional intelligence:

1. **Label and validate emotions:** Help children identify and label their emotions accurately. Validate their feelings and teach them healthy ways to express and manage their emotions.

2. **Teach problem-solving skills:** Guide children in developing problem-solving skills to effectively deal with challenging situations. Encourage them to think critically, consider different perspectives, and explore various solutions.

3. **Promote empathy and understanding:** Teach children to empathize with others and understand different points of view. Encourage them to consider how their actions and words may impact others and foster a positive attitude towards inclusivity and respect.

4. **Encourage self-reflection:** Help children develop self-awareness by encouraging them to reflect on their thoughts, feelings, and actions. This self-reflection promotes personal growth and a positive attitude towards self-improvement.

Nurturing a positive attitude in children is a lifelong journey that requires patience, consistency, and a genuine commitment to their well-being. By implementing these strategies and techniques, we can help our children develop a positive attitude that will serve them well in all aspects of their lives. Remember, the attitudes we instill in our children today will shape the adults they become tomorrow.

Chapter 9

Attitude Intelligence in Interactions

9.1 Attitude and Empathy

Empathy is the ability to understand and share the feelings of others. It is a fundamental aspect of human interaction and plays a crucial role in building meaningful relationships. When it comes to attitude intelligence, empathy is an essential component that can greatly enhance our interactions with others and positively impact every aspect of our lives.

Having a strong sense of empathy allows us to connect with others on a deeper level. It enables us to understand their perspectives, emotions, and experiences, which in turn helps us to respond in a more compassionate and considerate manner. By cultivating empathy, we can develop a greater understanding of the people around us, fostering stronger relationships and creating a more harmonious environment.

In personal relationships, empathy is vital for building trust and intimacy. When we empathize with our loved ones, we can better understand their needs, desires, and struggles. This understanding allows us to provide the support and care they require, strengthening the bond between us. By demonstrating empathy, we create a safe space for open communication and emotional vulnerability, which is essential for maintaining healthy and fulfilling relationships.

In professional life, empathy is equally important. It enables us to understand the perspectives and needs of our colleagues, clients, and customers. By putting ourselves in their shoes, we can tailor our communication and actions to meet their expectations effectively. This not only enhances teamwork and collaboration but also improves customer satisfaction and loyalty. Empathy in the workplace fosters a positive and inclusive environment, where individuals feel valued and understood.

Empathy also plays a significant role in our health and well-being. When we empathize with others, we develop a sense of interconnectedness and compassion. This can have a profound impact on our mental and emotional well-being, reducing stress and promoting a positive outlook on life. Additionally, empathy can enhance our physical health by encouraging us to engage in acts of kindness and support, which have been shown to boost the immune system and improve overall health.

In personal development, empathy helps us to understand ourselves better and develop a stronger sense of self-awareness. By empathizing with our own emotions and experiences, we can identify areas for growth and work towards personal improvement. Furthermore, empathy towards others allows us to learn from their experiences and gain valuable insights that can contribute to our own development. By embracing empathy, we open ourselves up to new perspectives and opportunities for growth.

Attitude intelligence combined with empathy can also have a significant impact on our financial success. By empathizing with others, we can better understand their needs and desires, which can inform our decision-making processes. This understanding can help us identify opportunities for innovation and create products or services that truly meet the needs of our target audience. Additionally, empathy can enhance our negotiation skills, allowing us to build mutually beneficial relationships and secure favorable outcomes.

In education, empathy is crucial for effective teaching and learning. When educators empathize with their students, they can better understand their individual strengths, weaknesses, and learning styles. This understanding enables them to tailor their teaching methods and provide personalized support, leading to improved academic performance and engagement. Furthermore, empathy in education fosters a positive and inclusive learning environment, where students feel valued and supported.

In parenting, empathy is essential for nurturing healthy parent-child relationships. By empathizing with our children, we can better understand their emotions and needs, allowing us to respond in a sensitive and supportive manner. This fosters a strong bond between parent and child, promoting trust, open communication, and emotional well-being. Additionally, empathy helps parents to teach important values such as kindness, compassion, and respect.

In social interactions, empathy is a powerful tool for building connections and fostering understanding between individuals from different backgrounds and cultures. By empathizing with others, we can bridge the gap of differences and promote cultural sensitivity. This leads to a more inclusive and harmonious society, where diversity is celebrated, and prejudice is challenged.

In conclusion, empathy is a vital component of attitude intelligence that has the power to positively impact every aspect of our lives. By cultivating empathy, we can build stronger relationships, enhance our communication skills, and create a more compassionate and inclusive world. Empathy allows us to understand and connect with others on a deeper level, fostering understanding, trust, and mutual respect. By embracing empathy, we can truly harness the power of attitude intelligence and create a more harmonious and fulfilling life.

9.2 Building Connections with Attitude Intelligence

Building connections with others is an essential aspect of our lives. Whether it's in our personal relationships, professional interactions, or social engagements, the ability to connect with others on a meaningful level can greatly impact our overall well-being and success. Attitude intelligence plays a crucial role in building these connections, as it allows us to approach interactions with a positive and open mindset, fostering understanding, empathy, and collaboration.

The Power of Attitude in Building Connections

Our attitude is the lens through which we perceive the world and interact with others. It shapes our thoughts, emotions, and behaviors, ultimately influencing the quality of our relationships. When we approach connections with a positive attitude, we create an environment that is conducive to building trust, respect, and mutual understanding.

Attitude intelligence enables us to cultivate a mindset that values and appreciates the uniqueness of others. It encourages us to be open-minded, non-judgmental, and empathetic, allowing us to connect with people from diverse backgrounds and perspectives. By embracing a positive attitude, we can bridge gaps, break down barriers, and foster meaningful connections with others.

Developing Attitude Intelligence for Building Connections

Developing attitude intelligence requires self-awareness, self-reflection, and a willingness to grow. Here are some strategies to enhance your attitude intelligence and build connections with others:

1. Practice Active Listening

Active listening is a fundamental skill in building connections. It involves giving your full attention to the person speaking, without interrupting or judging. By actively listening, you demonstrate respect and empathy, making the other person feel valued and understood. This creates a strong foundation for building connections based on trust and mutual respect.

2. Cultivate Empathy

Empathy is the ability to understand and share the feelings of others. It allows us to connect with others on a deeper level, as we can relate to their experiences and emotions. Cultivating empathy involves putting yourself in someone else's shoes, actively seeking to understand their perspective, and responding with compassion. By practicing empathy, you can build stronger connections and foster a sense of belonging.

3. Be Authentic and Genuine

Authenticity is key to building genuine connections. When you are true to yourself and express your thoughts and emotions honestly, others are more likely to trust and connect with you. Avoid putting on a facade or pretending to be someone you're not. Embrace your uniqueness and let your true self shine through in your interactions with others.

4. Show Appreciation and Gratitude

Expressing appreciation and gratitude towards others is a powerful way to build connections. Acknowledge and recognize the contributions and efforts of those around you. A simple thank you or a genuine compliment can go a long way in strengthening relationships and fostering a positive atmosphere.

5. Practice Effective Communication

Effective communication is essential for building connections. Be mindful of your tone, body language, and choice of words when interacting with others. Strive to be clear, concise, and respectful in your communication. Listen actively, ask clarifying questions, and provide constructive feedback when necessary. Effective communication builds trust and understanding, facilitating stronger connections.

6. Seek Common Ground

Finding common ground with others is an effective way to build connections. Look for shared interests, values, or goals that you can connect on. Engage in conversations that allow you to explore these commonalities and build rapport. By focusing on shared experiences, you can create a sense of belonging and strengthen your connections with others.

The Benefits of Building Connections with Attitude Intelligence

Building connections with attitude intelligence has numerous benefits that positively impact various aspects of our lives:

1. Enhanced Personal Relationships

Attitude intelligence strengthens personal relationships by fostering understanding, empathy, and effective communication. It allows us to connect with our loved ones on a deeper level, leading to stronger bonds and more fulfilling relationships.

2. Improved Professional Interactions

In the professional realm, attitude intelligence enables us to build positive relationships with colleagues, clients, and superiors. It promotes collaboration, teamwork, and effective communication, leading to increased productivity and career success.

3. Increased Social Engagement

Attitude intelligence enhances our ability to connect with others in social settings. It allows us to engage in meaningful conversations, build new friendships, and create a sense of community. By fostering connections, we can enrich our social lives and create a support network.

4. Enhanced Emotional Well-being

Building connections with a positive attitude contributes to our emotional well-being. Meaningful connections provide a sense of belonging, support, and validation, reducing feelings of loneliness and isolation. They also contribute to increased happiness, self-esteem, and overall life satisfaction.

5. Expanded Perspectives and Growth

Building connections with diverse individuals exposes us to different perspectives, ideas, and experiences. This broadens our horizons, promotes personal growth, and challenges our preconceived notions. Attitude intelligence allows us to embrace these differences and learn from others, fostering personal and intellectual development.

In conclusion, attitude intelligence plays a vital role in building connections with others. By cultivating a positive attitude, practicing active listening, empathy, and effective communication, we can foster meaningful relationships in all aspects of our lives. Building connections with attitude intelligence enhances our personal relationships, professional interactions, social engagements, and overall well-being. Embrace the power of attitude intelligence and watch as your connections flourish and enrich your life.

9.3 Attitude and Cultural Sensitivity

Cultural sensitivity is an essential aspect of attitude intelligence. It involves being aware of and respecting the beliefs, values, customs, and traditions of different cultures. Having a culturally sensitive attitude allows individuals to interact and communicate effectively with people from diverse backgrounds, fostering understanding, harmony, and inclusivity.

Understanding Cultural Sensitivity

Cultural sensitivity is the ability to recognize and appreciate the differences and similarities between various cultures. It involves being open-minded, non-judgmental, and willing to learn about different cultural practices and perspectives. Culturally sensitive individuals understand that there is no universal standard for behavior, and what may be acceptable in one culture may not be in another.

The Importance of Cultural Sensitivity

Cultural sensitivity is crucial in today's interconnected world. As globalization continues to bring people from different cultures together, it is essential to develop an attitude that embraces diversity and promotes inclusivity. Here are some reasons why cultural sensitivity is important:

1. **Promoting Respect and Understanding**: Cultural sensitivity helps to foster respect and understanding between individuals from different cultural backgrounds. It allows people to appreciate and value the diversity of human experiences, promoting empathy and reducing prejudice.

2. **Effective Communication**: Cultural sensitivity enhances communication by enabling individuals to understand and interpret verbal and non-verbal cues within a cultural context. It helps to avoid misunderstandings, misinterpretations, and potential conflicts that may arise due to cultural differences.

3. **Building Relationships**: Culturally sensitive individuals are more likely to build meaningful and authentic relationships with people from different cultures. By demonstrating respect for cultural practices and beliefs, they create an environment of trust and acceptance, which strengthens interpersonal connections.

4. **Enhancing Collaboration**: In professional settings, cultural sensitivity is crucial for effective collaboration and teamwork. It allows individuals to appreciate diverse perspectives, leverage different strengths, and work together towards common goals, leading to increased productivity and innovation.

5. **Avoiding Stereotypes and Prejudice**: Cultural sensitivity helps to challenge stereotypes and prejudices by recognizing the uniqueness of individuals within a cultural group. It encourages individuals to see beyond generalizations and treat

each person as an individual with their own beliefs, values, and experiences.

Developing Cultural Sensitivity

Developing cultural sensitivity is an ongoing process that requires self-reflection, education, and exposure to different cultures. Here are some strategies to enhance cultural sensitivity:

1. **Self-Awareness**: Start by examining your own cultural biases and assumptions. Reflect on how your own cultural background influences your attitudes and behaviors. Recognize that cultural sensitivity is a lifelong learning journey.

2. **Education and Learning**: Educate yourself about different cultures through books, documentaries, and online resources. Attend cultural events, festivals, and workshops to gain firsthand knowledge and understanding.

3. **Active Listening**: Practice active listening when engaging with individuals from different cultures. Pay attention to their perspectives, experiences, and values. Avoid making assumptions or imposing your own cultural norms.

4. **Respect and Empathy**: Show respect and empathy towards individuals from different cultures. Be open-minded and non-judgmental. Seek to understand their viewpoints and experiences without imposing your own beliefs.

5. **Ask Questions**: If you are unsure about a cultural practice or belief, ask questions respectfully. People are often willing to share their cultural experiences and appreciate genuine curiosity.

6. **Adaptability**: Be adaptable and flexible in different cultural settings. Recognize that cultural norms and practices may vary, and be willing to adjust your behavior accordingly.

7. **Avoid Stereotyping**: Challenge stereotypes and avoid making

generalizations about individuals based on their cultural background. Treat each person as an individual with their own unique experiences and perspectives.

Benefits of Cultural Sensitivity

Developing cultural sensitivity brings numerous benefits to individuals and society as a whole. Some of the key benefits include:

1. **Enhanced Interpersonal Relationships**: Culturally sensitive individuals are more likely to build strong and meaningful relationships with people from diverse backgrounds. They can connect on a deeper level and appreciate the richness of different cultures.

2. **Global Perspective**: Cultural sensitivity broadens one's perspective and understanding of the world. It allows individuals to see beyond their own cultural bubble and appreciate the diversity and complexity of human experiences.

3. **Reduced Conflict**: By promoting understanding and respect, cultural sensitivity helps to reduce conflicts that may arise due to cultural misunderstandings. It fosters an environment of harmony and inclusivity.

4. **Increased Creativity and Innovation**: Embracing diverse perspectives and ideas from different cultures stimulates creativity and innovation. Culturally sensitive individuals can draw inspiration from various cultural practices and adapt them to solve problems and create new solutions.

5. **Social Cohesion**: Cultural sensitivity contributes to social cohesion by promoting inclusivity and reducing discrimination. It helps to create a society where individuals from different cultural backgrounds can live harmoniously and contribute to the overall well-being of the community.

In conclusion, attitude intelligence encompasses cultural sensitivity as a vital component. Developing a culturally sensitive attitude allows individuals to navigate diverse cultural landscapes with respect, understanding, and empathy. By embracing cultural differences, we can foster inclusive relationships, effective communication, and a harmonious society.

9.4 Promoting Positive Attitude in Society

Promoting a positive attitude in society is crucial for creating a harmonious and thriving community. Attitude intelligence plays a significant role in shaping the collective mindset and behavior of individuals within a society. When individuals possess a positive attitude, it not only benefits their personal well-being but also has a ripple effect on the people around them. In this section, we will explore how promoting a positive attitude in society can lead to various positive outcomes and contribute to the overall growth and development of communities.

The Power of Positive Attitude in Society

A positive attitude has the power to transform societies by fostering a sense of unity, cooperation, and resilience. When individuals approach life with optimism and a can-do attitude, they are more likely to overcome challenges and find innovative solutions to societal problems. Positive attitudes also promote inclusivity and empathy, creating a supportive environment where individuals feel valued and understood.

Building a Positive Attitude Culture

Promoting a positive attitude in society requires a collective effort from individuals, communities, and institutions. Here are some strategies to build a positive attitude culture:

1. **Education and Awareness:** Educating individuals about the importance of a positive attitude and its impact on society is crucial. Schools, colleges, and community organizations can

incorporate attitude intelligence programs into their curriculum to teach young people about the benefits of positivity and how it can contribute to a better society.

2. **Role Models and Inspirational Figures:** Highlighting individuals who exemplify a positive attitude can inspire others to adopt similar mindsets. Sharing stories of resilience, compassion, and determination can motivate individuals to embrace positivity and make a difference in their communities.

3. **Promoting Emotional Intelligence:** Emotional intelligence is closely linked to attitude intelligence. By promoting emotional intelligence skills such as self-awareness, empathy, and effective communication, society can foster a positive and supportive environment where individuals can thrive.

4. **Encouraging Volunteerism and Community Engagement:** Engaging in volunteer activities and community service can cultivate a positive attitude by fostering a sense of purpose and connection. Encouraging individuals to contribute their time and skills to help others not only benefits the recipients but also enhances the well-being and satisfaction of the volunteers.

5. **Creating Supportive Networks:** Establishing support networks and platforms where individuals can connect, share experiences, and provide emotional support can contribute to a positive attitude culture. These networks can be created through community centers, online forums, or social media groups, allowing individuals to uplift and inspire each other.

The Benefits of Promoting Positive Attitude in Society

Promoting a positive attitude in society can have numerous benefits that extend beyond individual well-being. Here are some key advantages:

1. **Improved Mental Health:** A positive attitude can help

reduce stress, anxiety, and depression in individuals. By promoting a positive attitude in society, we can create an environment that supports mental well-being and encourages individuals to seek help when needed.

2. **Enhanced Social Connections:** A positive attitude fosters healthy relationships and social connections. When individuals approach interactions with positivity and kindness, it creates a ripple effect, leading to stronger social bonds and a sense of belonging within the community.

3. **Increased Productivity and Innovation:** A positive attitude promotes creativity, problem-solving, and a growth mindset. When individuals believe in their abilities and approach challenges with optimism, they are more likely to find innovative solutions and contribute to the overall progress and development of society.

4. **Reduced Conflict and Improved Cooperation:** A positive attitude encourages open-mindedness, empathy, and understanding. This leads to reduced conflicts and improved cooperation among individuals and groups within society. By promoting a positive attitude, we can create a more peaceful and harmonious community.

5. **Inspiration for Future Generations:** When society promotes a positive attitude, it sets an example for future generations. Children and young people who grow up in a positive attitude culture are more likely to adopt similar mindsets and contribute positively to society as they mature.

Overcoming Challenges in Promoting Positive Attitude

Promoting a positive attitude in society is not without its challenges. Here are some common obstacles and strategies to overcome them:

1. **Resistance to Change:** Some individuals may resist adopting

a positive attitude due to personal beliefs, past experiences, or cultural factors. Overcoming this resistance requires patience, empathy, and providing evidence of the benefits of positivity through success stories and scientific research.

2. **Negative Influences:** Negative influences, such as media portrayals, societal norms, and peer pressure, can hinder the promotion of a positive attitude. Counteracting these influences requires creating alternative narratives, promoting positive role models, and providing platforms for positive voices to be heard.

3. **Lack of Awareness:** Many individuals may not be aware of the impact of their attitude on society or may not have access to resources that promote a positive attitude. Raising awareness through education, community programs, and media campaigns can help bridge this gap.

4. **Sustainability:** Promoting a positive attitude in society requires long-term commitment and sustainability. It is essential to integrate attitude intelligence programs into various aspects of society, including education, workplaces, and community organizations, to ensure continuous reinforcement of positive attitudes.

By promoting a positive attitude in society, we can create a more compassionate, resilient, and thriving community. It is a collective responsibility to foster a positive attitude culture that benefits individuals, relationships, and the overall well-being of society. Let us embrace the power of attitude intelligence and work together to create a brighter future for all.

Chapter 10

Attitude Intelligence in Personal Happiness

10 .1 Attitude and Happiness

Happiness is a universal goal that transcends cultural boundaries and personal circumstances. It is a state of well-being and contentment that many people strive to achieve. Attitude intelligence plays a crucial role in determining our level of happiness and satisfaction in life. Our attitude towards ourselves, others, and the world around us greatly influences our overall happiness.

The Power of Attitude

Attitude is a mindset, a way of thinking and perceiving the world. It is the lens through which we interpret and respond to life's experiences. Our attitude shapes our thoughts, emotions, and actions, ultimately determining our happiness. A positive attitude allows us to approach life with optimism, resilience, and gratitude, while a negative attitude can lead to pessimism, dissatisfaction, and unhappiness.

The Link Between Attitude and Happiness

Research has consistently shown a strong correlation between attitude and happiness. Studies have found that individuals with a positive attitude tend to experience higher levels of happiness and life satisfaction. They are more resilient in the face of challenges, have better relationships, and enjoy better physical and mental health.

One reason for this link is that a positive attitude helps us focus on the good in life. It allows us to appreciate the present moment, find joy in simple pleasures, and cultivate gratitude for what we have. By adopting a positive attitude, we shift our perspective from dwelling on problems and negativity to embracing opportunities and possibilities.

Attitude and Emotional Well-being

Our attitude also plays a significant role in our emotional well-being. A positive attitude helps us manage stress, cope with adversity, and regulate our emotions effectively. It allows us to approach difficult situations with resilience and optimism, enabling us to bounce back from setbacks and maintain a sense of emotional balance.

On the other hand, a negative attitude can lead to emotional distress, such as anxiety, depression, and anger. When we constantly focus on the negative aspects of life, we become more susceptible to negative emotions and mental health issues. By cultivating a positive attitude, we can enhance our emotional well-being and experience greater happiness.

Cultivating a Positive Attitude for Happiness

Developing a positive attitude is a lifelong journey that requires conscious effort and self-reflection. Here are some strategies to cultivate a positive attitude and enhance happiness:

1. **Practice gratitude:** Cultivating gratitude is a powerful way to shift our focus towards the positive aspects of life. Take time each day to reflect on the things you are grateful for, whether big or small. This practice helps rewire our brains to notice and appreciate the good in our lives.

2. **Challenge negative thoughts:** Pay attention to your thoughts and challenge negative thinking patterns. Replace negative self-talk with positive affirmations and realistic perspectives. By reframing negative thoughts, you can cultivate a more positive attitude.

3. **Surround yourself with positivity:** Surround yourself with positive people who uplift and inspire you. Engage in activities that bring you joy and fulfillment. Create a positive environment that supports your happiness and well-being.

4. **Practice self-care:** Take care of your physical, mental, and emotional well-being. Engage in activities that promote self-care, such as exercise, meditation, and hobbies. Prioritize self-care to nurture a positive attitude and enhance your overall happiness.

5. **Focus on solutions:** Instead of dwelling on problems, focus on finding solutions. Adopt a proactive mindset that seeks opportunities for growth and improvement. By focusing on solutions, you can maintain a positive attitude even in challenging situations.

6. **Practice mindfulness:** Mindfulness is the practice of being fully present in the moment without judgment. It helps us cultivate awareness and acceptance of our thoughts, emotions, and experiences. By practicing mindfulness, we can develop a more positive attitude and experience greater happiness.

7. **Celebrate small victories:** Acknowledge and celebrate your achievements, no matter how small. Recognize your progress and give yourself credit for your efforts. Celebrating small victories boosts self-confidence and reinforces a positive attitude.

Remember, developing a positive attitude takes time and effort. It is a continuous practice that requires self-reflection, self-awareness, and a commitment to personal growth. By cultivating a positive attitude, you can enhance your happiness and create a more fulfilling life.

Conclusion

Attitude intelligence plays a vital role in our pursuit of happiness. By cultivating a positive attitude, we can enhance our overall well-being, improve our relationships, and navigate life's challenges with resilience and optimism. Happiness is not solely determined by external circumstances but is greatly influenced by our attitude towards life. Embracing a positive attitude is a powerful tool for creating a happier and more fulfilling life.

10.2 Gratitude and Attitude Intelligence

Gratitude is a powerful emotion that can significantly impact our attitude and overall well-being. When we cultivate an attitude of gratitude, we develop a deeper appreciation for the positive aspects of our lives, which in turn enhances our attitude intelligence. In this section, we will explore the connection between gratitude and attitude intelligence and how practicing gratitude can positively influence various aspects of our lives.

The Power of Gratitude

Gratitude is the practice of acknowledging and appreciating the good things in our lives. It involves recognizing the blessings, big or small, and expressing gratitude for them. When we adopt an attitude of gratitude, we shift our focus from what is lacking to what we have, fostering a positive mindset and enhancing our attitude intelligence.

Gratitude has been scientifically proven to have numerous benefits for our mental, emotional, and physical well-being. Research shows that practicing gratitude regularly can improve our mood, increase happiness levels, reduce stress and anxiety, enhance self-esteem, and even strengthen our immune system. By cultivating gratitude, we can transform our attitude and approach to life, leading to a more fulfilling and positive existence.

Gratitude and Attitude Intelligence

Attitude intelligence involves the ability to recognize and manage our attitudes effectively. It encompasses self-awareness, emotional intelligence, and the capacity to choose and maintain a positive attitude. Gratitude plays a vital role in developing and enhancing attitude intelligence by shifting our perspective and influencing our thoughts, emotions, and behaviors.

When we practice gratitude, we train our minds to focus on the positive aspects of our lives, even amidst challenges and difficulties. This shift in perspective allows us to approach situations with a more positive and optimistic attitude, enabling us to navigate through life's ups and downs with resilience and grace. Gratitude helps us reframe negative experiences, find lessons in setbacks, and appreciate the growth opportunities they present.

Gratitude in Personal Relationships

Gratitude has a profound impact on our personal relationships. When we express gratitude towards our loved ones, we strengthen the bond and deepen the connection. It fosters a sense of appreciation and acknowledgment, making the other person feel valued and loved. By practicing gratitude in our relationships, we create a positive and nurturing environment that promotes trust, understanding, and mutual support.

Furthermore, gratitude helps us focus on the positive qualities and actions of others, rather than dwelling on their flaws or shortcomings. This shift in perspective allows us to approach conflicts and disagreements with empathy and understanding, leading to more effective communication and resolution. Gratitude also encourages us to express our appreciation and gratitude to others, which can have a profound impact on their well-being and strengthen the relationship even further.

Gratitude in Professional Life

In the professional realm, gratitude can significantly impact our attitude intelligence and career success. When we cultivate gratitude in the workplace, we create a positive and supportive environment that fosters collaboration, teamwork, and productivity. Expressing gratitude towards our colleagues, subordinates, and superiors not only boosts their morale but also enhances our own job satisfaction and overall well-being.

Gratitude also helps us develop a growth mindset, which is essential for professional growth and success. By appreciating the opportunities, challenges, and lessons that come our way, we can approach our work with a positive and open attitude. This mindset allows us to embrace new experiences, learn from failures, and continuously improve our skills and knowledge.

Gratitude and Mental Well-being

Practicing gratitude has a profound impact on our mental well-being. It helps us shift our focus from negative thoughts and emotions to positive ones, reducing stress, anxiety, and depression. Gratitude promotes a sense of contentment and satisfaction, allowing us to appreciate the present moment and find joy in the simple pleasures of life.

Moreover, gratitude enhances our self-esteem and self-worth. When we acknowledge and appreciate the good things in our lives, we develop a more positive perception of ourselves. This positive self-image boosts our confidence and empowers us to overcome challenges and pursue our goals with determination and resilience.

Cultivating Gratitude

Cultivating gratitude is a practice that requires conscious effort and consistency. Here are some strategies to incorporate gratitude into your daily life:

1. Keep a gratitude journal: Write down three things you are grateful for each day. This practice helps you focus on the

positive aspects of your life and reinforces a grateful mindset.

2. Express gratitude to others: Take the time to express your appreciation and gratitude to the people around you. It can be a simple thank you note, a heartfelt conversation, or a small act of kindness.

3. Practice mindfulness: Be present in the moment and pay attention to the beauty and blessings around you. Mindfulness helps you cultivate gratitude by bringing your awareness to the present and fostering a sense of appreciation for the here and now.

4. Count your blessings: Take a moment each day to reflect on the things you are grateful for. It can be as simple as a roof over your head, a warm meal, or the love of your family and friends.

By incorporating these practices into your daily life, you can develop a habit of gratitude and enhance your attitude intelligence, leading to a more positive and fulfilling life.

In conclusion, gratitude and attitude intelligence are closely intertwined. Cultivating gratitude allows us to shift our perspective, enhance our attitude, and develop a positive mindset. By practicing gratitude in personal relationships, professional life, mental well-being, and various other aspects of our lives, we can harness the power of gratitude to enhance our attitude intelligence and lead a happier and more fulfilling life.

10.3 Mindfulness and Attitude

Mindfulness is a powerful practice that can greatly enhance our attitude intelligence and positively impact every aspect of our lives. It involves being fully present in the moment, paying attention to our thoughts, feelings, and sensations without judgment. By cultivating mindfulness, we can develop a deeper understanding of our attitudes and how they influence our experiences.

The Connection between Mindfulness and Attitude

Mindfulness and attitude are closely intertwined. When we practice mindfulness, we become more aware of our thoughts and emotions, allowing us to observe our attitudes more objectively. This awareness enables us to recognize any negative or unhelpful attitudes that may be holding us back and replace them with more positive and constructive ones.

By practicing mindfulness, we can also develop a greater sense of self-awareness. We become more attuned to our own patterns of thinking and reacting, allowing us to consciously choose our attitudes in different situations. This self-awareness empowers us to respond to challenges and setbacks with resilience and a positive mindset.

Mindfulness and Attitude in Personal Happiness

One of the key benefits of mindfulness is its ability to enhance personal happiness. When we practice mindfulness, we become more present in our lives and appreciate the simple joys and beauty around us. This shift in perspective allows us to cultivate a positive attitude towards life, focusing on gratitude and contentment rather than dwelling on negativity or dissatisfaction.

Mindfulness also helps us develop a non-judgmental attitude towards ourselves and others. Instead of criticizing or comparing, we learn to accept ourselves and others as we are, fostering compassion and empathy. This attitude of acceptance and kindness not only improves our relationships but also contributes to our overall happiness and well-being.

Mindfulness and Attitude in Relationships

Mindfulness plays a crucial role in fostering healthy and fulfilling relationships. When we practice mindfulness, we become more present and attentive to our loved ones. We listen more deeply, communicate more effectively, and respond with empathy and understanding. This mindful approach to relationships strengthens the bond between individuals and promotes a positive and harmonious atmosphere.

Moreover, mindfulness helps us become aware of our own attitudes and how they impact our interactions. We can observe any negative or reactive attitudes that may arise during conflicts or disagreements and consciously choose to respond with a more positive and compassionate attitude. This shift in attitude can transform conflicts into opportunities for growth and understanding.

Mindfulness and Attitude in Personal Development

In the realm of personal development, mindfulness is a valuable tool for enhancing attitude intelligence. By practicing mindfulness, we become more aware of our limiting beliefs and negative self-talk. We can observe these patterns without judgment and consciously choose to replace them with more empowering and positive attitudes.

Mindfulness also helps us develop a growth mindset, which is essential for personal growth and learning. With a growth mindset, we embrace challenges, view failures as opportunities for learning, and believe in our ability to improve and develop new skills. This positive attitude towards personal development enables us to overcome obstacles and achieve our goals.

Mindfulness and Attitude in Stress Management

Stress is an inevitable part of life, but our attitude towards stress can greatly influence its impact on our well-being. Mindfulness provides us with a powerful tool for managing stress by helping us cultivate a more positive and resilient attitude.

When we practice mindfulness, we become more aware of our stress triggers and how they affect us. We can observe our reactions and attitudes towards stress without judgment, allowing us to respond in a more calm and composed manner. Mindfulness also helps us develop a greater sense of perspective, enabling us to view stressful situations with a more balanced and positive attitude.

Cultivating Mindfulness for Attitude Intelligence

To cultivate mindfulness and enhance our attitude intelligence, we can incorporate various practices into our daily lives:

1. Meditation: Regular meditation practice allows us to develop mindfulness by focusing our attention on the present moment and observing our thoughts and emotions.
2. Mindful Breathing: Taking a few moments throughout the day to focus on our breath can help us anchor ourselves in the present moment and cultivate mindfulness.
3. Body Scan: Engaging in a body scan practice involves systematically bringing our attention to different parts of our body, promoting a sense of relaxation and mindfulness.
4. Mindful Eating: Paying attention to the taste, texture, and sensations of each bite during meals can help us cultivate mindfulness and develop a more positive attitude towards food.
5. Mindful Movement: Engaging in activities such as yoga, tai chi, or walking meditation can help us cultivate mindfulness by bringing our attention to the physical sensations and movements of our bodies.

By incorporating these practices into our daily routines, we can gradually develop a greater sense of mindfulness and enhance our attitude intelligence in every aspect of our lives.

Conclusion

Mindfulness is a transformative practice that can significantly enhance our attitude intelligence. By cultivating mindfulness, we become more aware of our attitudes and how they influence our experiences. Mindfulness helps us develop a positive and compassionate attitude towards ourselves and others, fostering personal happiness and healthy relationships. It also enhances our personal development, stress management, and overall well-being. By incorporating mindfulness practices into our daily lives, we can cultivate a deeper sense of mindfulness and unlock the full potential of our attitude intelligence.

10.4 Finding Joy through Attitude Intelligence

Attitude Intelligence plays a crucial role in finding joy and happiness in every aspect of life. Our attitude shapes our perception, reactions, and overall experience of the world around us. By cultivating a positive and optimistic attitude, we can enhance our ability to find joy and create a fulfilling life.

The Power of a Positive Attitude

A positive attitude is a key ingredient in finding joy and happiness. It allows us to approach life's challenges with resilience, optimism, and a solution-oriented mindset. When we maintain a positive attitude, we are better equipped to navigate through difficult situations and find joy even in the face of adversity.

Having a positive attitude also helps us to appreciate the present moment and find joy in the simple pleasures of life. It allows us to focus on the good things rather than dwelling on the negative aspects. By adopting a positive mindset, we can shift our perspective and find joy in even the smallest of things.

Cultivating Gratitude

Gratitude is another essential aspect of finding joy through attitude intelligence. When we practice gratitude, we shift our focus from what is lacking in our lives to what we already have. It helps us to appreciate the blessings, big or small, and find joy in the abundance that surrounds us.

By incorporating gratitude into our daily lives, we train our minds to notice and acknowledge the positive aspects of our experiences. This practice helps us to cultivate a positive attitude and find joy in the present moment. Whether it's expressing gratitude for the love and support of our loved ones or appreciating the beauty of nature, gratitude opens the door to joy and happiness.

Embracing Mindfulness

Mindfulness is the practice of being fully present and aware of the present moment without judgment. It involves paying attention to our thoughts, feelings, and sensations in a non-reactive manner. By practicing mindfulness, we can cultivate a deeper sense of joy and contentment in our lives.

When we are mindful, we become more attuned to the beauty and wonder of the present moment. We can fully engage in our experiences, whether it's savoring a delicious meal, enjoying a walk in nature, or spending quality time with loved ones. By being fully present, we can find joy in the simple pleasures that often go unnoticed.

Choosing Joy

Attitude intelligence empowers us to choose joy in every situation. While we cannot control external circumstances, we have the power to control our attitude and how we respond to them. By consciously choosing a positive and joyful attitude, we can transform even the most challenging situations into opportunities for growth and happiness.

Choosing joy also involves letting go of negativity and embracing forgiveness. Holding onto grudges and negative emotions only weighs us down and prevents us from experiencing true joy. By practicing forgiveness, we free ourselves from the burden of resentment and create space for joy to enter our lives.

Finding Joy in Relationships

Attitude intelligence also plays a significant role in our relationships. By cultivating a positive attitude, we can enhance our connections with others and find joy in the bonds we share. A positive attitude allows us to approach relationships with empathy, compassion, and understanding, fostering a sense of joy and fulfillment in our interactions.

When we maintain a positive attitude in our relationships, we can appreciate the unique qualities and contributions of others. We can celebrate their successes, support them during challenging times, and find joy in the shared experiences and memories we create together.

Pursuing Passions and Purpose

Attitude intelligence encourages us to pursue our passions and live a life aligned with our purpose. When we engage in activities that bring us joy and fulfillment, we enhance our overall well-being and sense of happiness. By following our passions, we infuse our lives with a sense of purpose and meaning, which in turn brings us joy.

When we approach our passions with a positive attitude, we can overcome obstacles and setbacks with resilience and determination. We can find joy in the process of growth and learning, rather than solely focusing on the end result. By pursuing our passions and living a purpose-driven life, we create opportunities for joy and fulfillment to flourish.

Conclusion

Attitude intelligence is a powerful tool for finding joy and happiness in every aspect of life. By cultivating a positive attitude, practicing gratitude, embracing mindfulness, and choosing joy, we can enhance our overall well-being and create a life filled with joy and fulfillment. Through our attitude, we have the power to shape our experiences and find joy in even the simplest of moments. So, let us embrace the power of attitude intelligence and embark on a journey of joy and happiness.

Chapter 11

Attitude Intelligence in Overcoming Challenges

11.1 Attitude and Resilience
Resilience is the ability to bounce back from adversity, to adapt and recover quickly from difficult situations. It is a crucial trait that can greatly impact our ability to overcome challenges and achieve success in various aspects of life. Attitude intelligence plays a significant role in developing and maintaining resilience.

Attitude and resilience are closely intertwined. Our attitude, or the way we think and perceive situations, greatly influences how we respond to adversity. A positive attitude can help us view challenges as opportunities for growth and learning, while a negative attitude can hinder our ability to bounce back and find solutions.

One of the key aspects of attitude intelligence is the ability to maintain a positive mindset in the face of adversity. It involves cultivating a belief in our own abilities and strengths, as well as having confidence in our capacity to overcome obstacles. A positive attitude allows us to approach challenges with optimism and determination, which in turn enhances our resilience.

When faced with setbacks or failures, individuals with high attitude intelligence are more likely to view them as temporary and specific to the situation, rather than as a reflection of their overall abilities or worth. They understand that setbacks are a natural part of life and see them as opportunities for growth and self-improvement. This mindset enables them to bounce back quickly and find alternative solutions to overcome obstacles.

Attitude intelligence also involves developing emotional resilience. It is the ability to manage and regulate our emotions effectively, especially during challenging times. Emotionally resilient individuals are better equipped to handle stress, disappointment, and frustration without becoming overwhelmed or giving up. They are able to maintain a positive attitude and focus on finding solutions rather than dwelling on negative emotions.

Furthermore, attitude intelligence helps us develop a flexible mindset. It allows us to adapt to changing circumstances and embrace new challenges with an open mind. Resilient individuals understand that life is full of uncertainties and that the ability to adapt and adjust is crucial for success. They are willing to step out of their comfort zones, take risks, and explore new possibilities.

Attitude intelligence also plays a vital role in problem-solving. Resilient individuals approach problems with a positive attitude and a belief that they have the ability to find solutions. They are not easily discouraged by setbacks or obstacles but instead see them as opportunities to think creatively and find innovative solutions. Their positive attitude fuels their determination and perseverance, enabling them to overcome even the most difficult challenges.

In addition, attitude intelligence helps us develop a growth mindset. This mindset is characterized by the belief that our abilities and intelligence can be developed through dedication and hard work. Individuals with a growth mindset see failures and setbacks as opportunities for learning and improvement. They embrace challenges and view them as stepping stones towards personal and professional growth. This mindset enhances resilience by fostering a belief in our ability to learn from mistakes and adapt to new situations.

Attitude intelligence also enables us to build a strong support network. Resilient individuals understand the importance of surrounding themselves with positive and supportive people. They seek out individuals who inspire and motivate them, and who can provide guidance and encouragement during challenging times. Building a strong support network helps us maintain a positive attitude and provides us with the necessary emotional support to bounce back from adversity.

In conclusion, attitude intelligence plays a crucial role in developing and maintaining resilience. A positive attitude, emotional resilience, flexibility, problem-solving skills, and a growth mindset are all key components of attitude intelligence that contribute to our ability to overcome challenges and bounce back from adversity. By cultivating attitude intelligence, we can enhance our resilience and navigate through life's ups and downs with strength and determination.

11.2 Positive Attitude in Times of Adversity

In life, we all face challenges and adversities. Whether it's a personal setback, a professional obstacle, or a global crisis, adversity is an inevitable part of the human experience. However, what sets individuals apart is their ability to maintain a positive attitude in the face of adversity. This is where attitude intelligence plays a crucial role.

Positive attitude in times of adversity is not about denying or ignoring the difficulties we encounter. It is about approaching challenges with resilience, optimism, and a growth mindset. It is about finding the silver lining, learning from setbacks, and using them as stepping stones for personal growth and development.

The Power of Positive Attitude

A positive attitude is a powerful tool that can help us navigate through the toughest of times. It allows us to maintain a sense of hope, optimism, and determination, even when the odds are stacked against us. Research has shown that individuals with a positive attitude are more likely to overcome obstacles, bounce back from failures, and achieve success in various areas of life.

When faced with adversity, a positive attitude can help us in several ways:

1. **Emotional Resilience:** A positive attitude helps us build emotional resilience, enabling us to cope with stress, anxiety, and negative emotions more effectively. It allows us to maintain a sense of calm and composure, even in the face of challenging circumstances.

2. **Problem-Solving:** A positive attitude enhances our problem-solving skills. It helps us approach problems with a proactive mindset, seeking solutions rather than dwelling on the difficulties. With a positive attitude, we are more likely to find creative and innovative solutions to overcome obstacles.

3. **Motivation and Persistence:** Adversity can often lead to feelings of demotivation and giving up. However, a positive attitude fuels our motivation and persistence. It helps us stay focused on our goals, maintain a sense of purpose, and keep pushing forward, even when the going gets tough.

4. **Improved Relationships:** A positive attitude not only benefits us individually but also has a positive impact on our

relationships. When we approach adversity with a positive mindset, we are more likely to seek support, collaborate with others, and build stronger connections. This support system can provide us with the encouragement and assistance we need to overcome challenges.

Cultivating a Positive Attitude in Times of Adversity

While maintaining a positive attitude in times of adversity may not always be easy, it is a skill that can be developed and strengthened with practice. Here are some strategies to cultivate a positive attitude:

1. **Practice Gratitude:** Expressing gratitude for the things we have, even in difficult times, can shift our focus from what's going wrong to what's going right. Take a few moments each day to reflect on the things you are grateful for, no matter how small they may seem.

2. **Reframe Negative Thoughts:** Challenge negative thoughts and replace them with more positive and empowering ones. Instead of dwelling on what went wrong, focus on what you can learn from the situation and how it can contribute to your personal growth.

3. **Seek Support:** Surround yourself with positive and supportive individuals who can uplift you during challenging times. Share your thoughts and feelings with trusted friends, family members, or mentors who can provide guidance and encouragement.

4. **Practice Self-Care:** Taking care of your physical, mental, and emotional well-being is crucial in maintaining a positive attitude. Engage in activities that bring you joy, practice mindfulness or meditation, exercise regularly, and ensure you get enough rest and relaxation.

5. **Set Realistic Goals:** Break down your challenges into smaller, manageable goals. Celebrate each small victory along the way,

as it will boost your confidence and reinforce your positive attitude.

6. **Learn from Adversity:** View adversity as an opportunity for growth and learning. Reflect on the lessons you can take away from the experience and how it can shape you into a stronger and more resilient individual.

7. **Practice Positive Self-Talk:** Be mindful of your inner dialogue and replace self-critical thoughts with positive affirmations. Remind yourself of your strengths, capabilities, and past successes.

Remember, maintaining a positive attitude in times of adversity is not about denying the difficulties or pretending everything is fine. It is about acknowledging the challenges, accepting them, and choosing to respond in a way that empowers and uplifts you. By cultivating a positive attitude, you can navigate through adversity with grace, resilience, and a renewed sense of purpose.

11.3 Attitude and Problem-Solving

Problem-solving is an essential skill that we all need in our lives. Whether it's overcoming personal challenges, navigating professional obstacles, or finding solutions to complex issues, having the right attitude can greatly impact our problem-solving abilities. Attitude intelligence plays a crucial role in how we approach and tackle problems, allowing us to find effective and innovative solutions. In this section, we will explore the connection between attitude and problem-solving and how cultivating a positive attitude can enhance our problem-solving skills.

The Power of a Positive Attitude in Problem-Solving

Attitude is a mindset that shapes our thoughts, emotions, and actions. When it comes to problem-solving, having a positive attitude can make a significant difference in our ability to find solutions. A positive attitude enables us to approach problems with optimism, resilience, and a belief in our ability to overcome challenges. It allows us to see setbacks as opportunities for growth and learning, rather than insurmountable obstacles.

A positive attitude also helps us maintain a solution-oriented mindset. Instead of dwelling on the problem itself, we focus on finding ways to solve it. This mindset encourages creativity, flexibility, and open-mindedness, enabling us to explore different perspectives and consider unconventional approaches. With a positive attitude, we are more likely to persevere through difficulties, adapt to changing circumstances, and find innovative solutions.

Developing an Attitude for Effective Problem-Solving

Cultivating an attitude that supports effective problem-solving requires self-awareness, mindset shifts, and intentional practice. Here are some strategies to develop an attitude that enhances problem-solving skills:

1. Embrace a Growth Mindset

A growth mindset is the belief that our abilities and intelligence can be developed through dedication and hard work. Embracing a growth mindset allows us to view challenges as opportunities for growth and learning. Instead of being discouraged by setbacks, we see them as stepping stones towards improvement. By adopting a growth mindset, we become more resilient, adaptable, and open to new ideas, all of which are essential for effective problem-solving.

2. Foster a Solution-Oriented Attitude

A solution-oriented attitude focuses on finding answers rather than dwelling on problems. It involves reframing challenges as opportunities and actively seeking solutions. To foster a solution-oriented attitude, practice reframing negative thoughts into positive ones. Instead of saying, "This problem is impossible to solve," shift your mindset to, "There must be a solution, and I will find it." By training your mind to focus on solutions, you will become more proactive and resourceful in your problem-solving approach.

3. Cultivate Resilience and Perseverance

Resilience is the ability to bounce back from setbacks and maintain a positive attitude in the face of adversity. It is a crucial trait for effective problem-solving. Cultivate resilience by developing coping mechanisms, such as practicing self-care, seeking support from others, and reframing failures as learning opportunities. By building resilience, you will be better equipped to handle challenges, stay motivated, and persist in finding solutions.

4. Practice Creative and Critical Thinking

Creative and critical thinking are essential skills for effective problem-solving. Creative thinking involves generating new ideas, exploring different perspectives, and thinking outside the box. Critical thinking, on the other hand, involves analyzing information, evaluating options, and making informed decisions. To enhance these skills, engage in activities that stimulate your creativity, such as brainstorming sessions, mind mapping, or seeking diverse viewpoints. Additionally, practice analyzing problems from different angles, considering potential consequences, and weighing the pros and cons of various solutions.

5. Maintain a Positive and Optimistic Outlook

A positive and optimistic outlook is a key component of attitude intelligence in problem-solving. It helps us maintain motivation, resilience, and a belief in our ability to find solutions. To cultivate a positive outlook, practice gratitude, focus on the positives in every situation, and surround yourself with positive influences. Engage in activities that uplift your mood, such as exercise, spending time in nature, or practicing mindfulness. By nurturing a positive mindset, you will approach problems with a can-do attitude and an unwavering belief in your ability to overcome challenges.

Applying Attitude Intelligence to Problem-Solving

Once you have developed an attitude that supports effective problem-solving, it's important to apply it in practical situations. Here are some tips for applying attitude intelligence to problem-solving:

1. Define the Problem Clearly

Before diving into finding solutions, take the time to define the problem clearly. Understand the root cause, identify the desired outcome, and break down the problem into smaller, manageable parts. By defining the problem clearly, you will be able to approach it with a focused and strategic mindset.

2. Generate Multiple Solutions

Avoid settling for the first solution that comes to mind. Instead, generate multiple solutions by brainstorming and considering different perspectives. Encourage creativity and think outside the box. Remember, there is often more than one way to solve a problem, and exploring various options can lead to innovative and effective solutions.

3. Evaluate and Select the Best Solution

Once you have a list of potential solutions, evaluate each one based on its feasibility, potential outcomes, and alignment with your goals. Consider the pros and cons of each solution and select the one that best addresses the problem while aligning with your values and priorities.

4. Take Action and Adapt as Needed

Implement your chosen solution and take action. Be prepared to adapt and make adjustments along the way. Problem-solving is rarely a linear process, and unforeseen challenges may arise. Maintain a flexible mindset and be willing to modify your approach if necessary.

5. Learn from the Process

Regardless of the outcome, view problem-solving as a learning opportunity. Reflect on the process, identify lessons learned, and apply them to future problem-solving situations. Continuous learning and improvement are essential for developing effective problem-solving skills.

By combining attitude intelligence with problem-solving techniques, you can approach challenges with confidence, creativity, and resilience. Remember, attitude is not just a passive state of mind; it is an active choice that can empower you to overcome obstacles and find solutions. Embrace a positive attitude, cultivate the necessary skills, and apply them consistently in your problem-solving endeavors.

11.4 Overcoming Fear with Attitude Intelligence

Fear is a natural human emotion that can often hold us back from reaching our full potential. It can manifest in various forms, such as fear of failure, fear of rejection, or fear of the unknown. However, with the right mindset and attitude intelligence, we can learn to overcome our fears and live a more fulfilling life.

Attitude intelligence plays a crucial role in overcoming fear. It involves developing a positive and resilient mindset that allows us to face our fears head-on and take action despite the discomfort. By cultivating the right attitude, we can transform fear into an opportunity for growth and personal development.

Understanding Fear

Before we can overcome fear, it is essential to understand its underlying causes and effects. Fear often stems from our perception of potential threats or negative outcomes. It is a natural response designed to protect us from harm. However, fear can become irrational and limit our ability to take risks or pursue our goals.

Fear can manifest in different ways, such as physical symptoms (racing heart, sweaty palms), emotional distress (anxiety, panic), or avoidance behaviors (procrastination, withdrawal). It can hold us back from trying new things, pursuing our passions, or taking necessary steps towards personal growth.

The Role of Attitude Intelligence

Attitude intelligence empowers us to reframe our perception of fear and approach it with a positive mindset. It involves developing self-awareness, emotional resilience, and a growth-oriented attitude. By cultivating these qualities, we can transform fear from a paralyzing force into a catalyst for personal growth and success.

1. **Self-Awareness:** Developing self-awareness is the first step in overcoming fear. By understanding our fears and their underlying causes, we can gain insight into how they affect our thoughts, emotions, and behaviors. Self-awareness allows us to identify the limiting beliefs and negative thought patterns that contribute to our fears.

2. **Emotional Resilience:** Building emotional resilience is crucial in managing fear. It involves developing the ability to regulate our emotions and bounce back from setbacks. With emotional resilience, we can acknowledge our fears without letting them control our actions. We can learn to tolerate discomfort and uncertainty, which are often associated with fear.

3. **Growth-Oriented Attitude:** Adopting a growth-oriented attitude is essential in overcoming fear. It involves embracing

challenges, viewing failures as learning opportunities, and believing in our ability to grow and adapt. With a growth mindset, we can reframe fear as a necessary part of the journey towards personal development and success.

Strategies for Overcoming Fear

Overcoming fear requires consistent effort and practice. Here are some strategies that can help you develop attitude intelligence and conquer your fears:

1. **Identify and Challenge Limiting Beliefs:** Start by identifying the limiting beliefs that contribute to your fears. Ask yourself if these beliefs are based on facts or if they are holding you back from reaching your goals. Challenge these beliefs by gathering evidence to support alternative perspectives and adopting more empowering beliefs.

2. **Take Small Steps:** Break down your fears into smaller, manageable steps. By taking small actions towards your goals, you can gradually build confidence and reduce the intensity of your fears. Celebrate each small victory along the way, as it will reinforce your belief in your ability to overcome challenges.

3. **Practice Mindfulness:** Mindfulness can help you develop a non-judgmental awareness of your fears and emotions. By observing your thoughts and feelings without attaching to them, you can create space for more rational and constructive thinking. Mindfulness also helps you stay present and focused, reducing the influence of future-oriented fears.

4. **Seek Support:** Surround yourself with a supportive network of friends, family, or mentors who can provide encouragement and guidance. Share your fears with trusted individuals who can offer a fresh perspective and help you stay accountable to your goals. Remember, you don't have to face your fears alone.

5. **Visualize Success:** Use the power of visualization to imagine

yourself successfully overcoming your fears. Visualize the positive outcomes and the feelings of accomplishment that come with conquering your fears. This technique can help rewire your brain to associate positive emotions with the actions you fear.

6. **Celebrate Progress:** Acknowledge and celebrate your progress, no matter how small. Recognize the courage it takes to face your fears and take action. By celebrating your achievements, you reinforce the belief that you are capable of overcoming any obstacle that comes your way.

Embracing a Fearless Attitude

Overcoming fear is a lifelong journey that requires continuous effort and self-reflection. Attitude intelligence provides us with the tools and mindset needed to face our fears head-on and live a life free from the limitations imposed by fear. By cultivating self-awareness, emotional resilience, and a growth-oriented attitude, we can transform fear into an opportunity for personal growth, success, and fulfillment.

Remember, fear is not something to be eliminated entirely but rather something to be understood and managed. With the right attitude, you can harness the power of fear and use it as a driving force towards achieving your goals and living a life of purpose and meaning. Embrace a fearless attitude, and watch as your potential unfolds before you.

Chapter 12

Conclusion

12 .1 Applying Attitude Intelligence in Everyday Life

Attitude intelligence is not limited to specific areas of life; it permeates every aspect of our existence. It is a mindset and a set of skills that can be applied to enhance our experiences and interactions in all areas of life. By cultivating attitude intelligence, we can navigate challenges, build meaningful relationships, achieve personal growth, and find fulfillment in our everyday lives.

Attitude Intelligence in Personal Relationships

Our attitude plays a crucial role in shaping our personal relationships. By applying attitude intelligence, we can foster healthy and meaningful connections with others. It starts with understanding the impact of our attitude on communication. Being aware of our tone, body language, and choice of words can significantly influence how our message is received.

Attitude intelligence also helps us build and maintain healthy relationships. By approaching interactions with empathy, respect, and understanding, we can create a positive environment that nurtures trust and mutual support. When conflicts arise, attitude intelligence allows us to approach them with a solution-oriented mindset, seeking resolutions that benefit all parties involved.

Attitude Intelligence in Professional Life

In the professional realm, attitude intelligence is a key factor in career success. Employers value individuals who demonstrate a positive attitude, as it contributes to a productive and harmonious work environment. By developing a winning attitude at work, we can enhance our performance, increase our chances of promotion, and build strong professional relationships.

Leadership and attitude intelligence go hand in hand. Effective leaders understand the impact of their attitude on their team's morale and productivity. By cultivating a positive and inspiring attitude, leaders can motivate their team members, foster a sense of belonging, and create an environment conducive to growth and innovation.

Managing stress and maintaining a positive attitude in the workplace is another crucial aspect of attitude intelligence. By developing resilience and adopting a positive mindset, we can navigate challenges and setbacks with grace and determination. This not only benefits our own well-being but also positively influences the overall work atmosphere.

Attitude intelligence also plays a vital role in professional growth. By embracing a continuous learning mindset and seeking opportunities for self-improvement, we can expand our knowledge and skills, opening doors to new possibilities and advancement in our careers. Additionally, maintaining a healthy work-life balance is essential for overall well-being, and attitude intelligence helps us prioritize and manage our time effectively.

Attitude Intelligence in Health and Well-being

Our attitude has a profound impact on our physical and mental health. Attitude intelligence allows us to cultivate a positive mindset that promotes overall well-being. By adopting a positive attitude towards our physical health, we can make healthier lifestyle choices, such as exercising regularly, eating nutritious food, and getting enough rest. This positive attitude towards our physical well-being can lead to increased energy levels, improved immune function, and a reduced risk of chronic diseases.

Mental well-being is equally important, and attitude intelligence plays a significant role in this aspect as well. By developing a positive attitude, we can cultivate resilience, manage stress effectively, and cope with challenges more efficiently. A positive attitude also enhances our emotional intelligence, allowing us to regulate our emotions, build stronger relationships, and experience greater happiness and fulfillment.

Attitude Intelligence in Personal Development

Attitude intelligence is a powerful tool for personal development. By adopting a positive attitude, we can boost our self-confidence and belief in our abilities. This self-assurance enables us to set and achieve meaningful goals, overcome obstacles, and embrace continuous learning.

Attitude intelligence helps us develop a growth mindset, which is essential for personal growth. By viewing challenges as opportunities for growth and learning, we can approach them with a positive attitude and a solution-oriented mindset. This mindset allows us to persevere in the face of adversity, learn from our mistakes, and continuously improve ourselves.

Attitude Intelligence in Financial Success

Attitude intelligence also plays a significant role in achieving financial success. Our attitude towards money and our financial mindset greatly influence our financial decisions and behaviors. By cultivating a positive attitude towards money, we can develop healthy financial habits, such as budgeting, saving, and investing wisely.

A positive attitude towards wealth and abundance allows us to attract opportunities and take calculated risks that can lead to financial growth. Attitude intelligence helps us make informed financial decisions by considering long-term goals, managing risks, and avoiding impulsive behaviors.

Attitude Intelligence in Education

Attitude intelligence is closely linked to academic success and lifelong learning. By adopting a positive attitude towards learning, we can enhance our motivation, focus, and perseverance. This positive attitude allows us to embrace challenges, seek knowledge, and develop a love for learning.

Attitude intelligence also helps us develop a growth mindset in education. By believing in our ability to learn and improve, we can overcome self-doubt and embrace continuous learning. This mindset enables us to approach new subjects and skills with enthusiasm and resilience, leading to greater academic achievements.

Attitude Intelligence in Parenting

Attitude intelligence is invaluable in parenting. By cultivating a positive attitude, parents can create a nurturing and supportive environment for their children. Attitude intelligence helps parents build strong parent-child relationships based on empathy, respect, and effective communication.

Positive discipline techniques, guided by attitude intelligence, allow parents to teach their children important values and life skills while fostering their emotional well-being. Attitude intelligence also helps parents teach resilience to their children, enabling them to face challenges, overcome obstacles, and develop a positive mindset.

Attitude Intelligence in Social Interactions

Attitude intelligence plays a crucial role in our social interactions. By adopting a positive attitude, we can build connections with others based on empathy, understanding, and respect. Attitude intelligence helps us appreciate and embrace cultural diversity, promoting inclusivity and harmony in society.

By promoting a positive attitude in our social interactions, we can inspire others to adopt a similar mindset. Attitude intelligence allows us to lead by example, spreading positivity, and creating a ripple effect of kindness and compassion in our communities.

Attitude Intelligence in Personal Happiness

Attitude intelligence is closely linked to personal happiness. By adopting a positive attitude, we can cultivate gratitude, mindfulness, and a sense of joy in our everyday lives. Attitude intelligence helps us appreciate the present moment, find beauty in simple pleasures, and maintain a positive outlook even in challenging times.

By applying attitude intelligence, we can overcome obstacles, develop resilience, and approach life with a solution-oriented mindset. This positive attitude allows us to find happiness and fulfillment in our relationships, careers, personal growth, and overall well-being.

Conclusion

Applying attitude intelligence in everyday life is a transformative practice that can enhance every aspect of our existence. By cultivating a positive attitude, we can navigate challenges, build meaningful relationships, achieve personal growth, and find happiness and fulfillment. Attitude intelligence is a lifelong journey that requires self-awareness, continuous learning, and a commitment to personal development. By embracing attitude intelligence, we not only improve our own lives but also inspire and positively influence those around us. The future of attitude intelligence holds the potential for a more compassionate, resilient, and harmonious world.

12.2 Continuing the Journey of Attitude Development

Attitude intelligence is not a destination; it is a lifelong journey of personal growth and development. Once you have started cultivating a positive attitude and harnessing the power of attitude intelligence, it is essential to continue nurturing and refining it in every aspect of your life. In this section, we will explore how you can continue your journey of attitude development and apply it to various areas of your life.

Embracing a Growth Mindset

One of the key elements of attitude intelligence is having a growth mindset. This mindset is characterized by the belief that your abilities and intelligence can be developed through dedication, effort, and a willingness to learn from failures and setbacks. By embracing a growth mindset, you open yourself up to endless possibilities for personal and professional growth.

To continue your journey of attitude development, it is crucial to consistently challenge yourself and seek opportunities for learning and self-improvement. This can involve taking on new projects at work, pursuing further education or certifications, or engaging in hobbies and activities that expand your knowledge and skills. By actively seeking growth opportunities, you not only enhance your attitude intelligence but also increase your chances of success and fulfillment in all areas of your life.

Cultivating Self-Awareness

Self-awareness is a fundamental aspect of attitude intelligence. It involves understanding your own thoughts, emotions, and behaviors, as well as their impact on yourself and others. By cultivating self-awareness, you can identify any negative attitudes or limiting beliefs that may be holding you back and work towards replacing them with more positive and empowering ones.

Continuing the journey of attitude development requires regular self-reflection and introspection. Take the time to examine your attitudes and beliefs, and ask yourself if they are serving you well or hindering your progress. Be honest with yourself and open to making necessary changes. This ongoing process of self-awareness will enable you to continually refine and improve your attitude intelligence.

Practicing Mindfulness

Mindfulness is the practice of being fully present in the moment, without judgment. It involves paying attention to your thoughts, feelings, and sensations, as well as the world around you. By incorporating mindfulness into your daily life, you can develop a deeper understanding of your attitudes and reactions, and consciously choose how to respond to different situations.

To continue your journey of attitude development, make mindfulness a regular part of your routine. Set aside dedicated time each day for mindfulness meditation or engage in activities that promote mindfulness, such as yoga or nature walks. By cultivating mindfulness, you can become more aware of your attitudes in real-time and make conscious choices to respond with positivity and resilience.

Seeking Feedback and Support

No journey of personal development is complete without seeking feedback and support from others. Surrounding yourself with positive and like-minded individuals who support your growth can greatly enhance your attitude intelligence. Seek out mentors, coaches, or trusted friends who can provide constructive feedback, guidance, and encouragement along the way.

Additionally, be open to receiving feedback from others, even if it may be challenging to hear. Constructive criticism can help you identify areas for improvement and refine your attitude intelligence. Embrace feedback as an opportunity for growth and use it to further develop your attitudes and behaviors.

Setting Meaningful Goals

Goal setting is a powerful tool for personal growth and development. By setting meaningful and achievable goals, you can direct your efforts and focus towards specific areas of attitude development. Whether it is improving your communication skills, enhancing your resilience, or cultivating a more positive mindset, setting goals provides a roadmap for your journey of attitude development.

When setting goals, ensure they are specific, measurable, attainable, relevant, and time-bound (SMART). Break down larger goals into smaller, manageable steps, and celebrate your progress along the way. Regularly review and adjust your goals as needed to stay aligned with your evolving attitude intelligence.

Embracing a Lifelong Learning Mindset

Attitude intelligence is not a one-time achievement; it requires a commitment to lifelong learning and growth. Embrace the mindset that there is always more to learn and discover. Stay curious and open-minded, seeking out new knowledge and perspectives that can further enhance your attitude intelligence.

Continuing the journey of attitude development involves actively seeking out opportunities for learning and personal growth. This can include attending workshops, seminars, or conferences, reading books or articles on personal development, or engaging in online courses or webinars. By investing in your ongoing education, you can continually expand your attitude intelligence and stay ahead in all areas of your life.

Conclusion

Continuing the journey of attitude development is a lifelong commitment to personal growth and self-improvement. By embracing a growth mindset, cultivating self-awareness, practicing mindfulness, seeking feedback and support, setting meaningful goals, and embracing a lifelong learning mindset, you can continue to refine and enhance your attitude intelligence in every aspect of your life.

Remember, attitude intelligence is not a destination but a continuous process of growth and development. Embrace the journey, stay committed to your personal growth, and inspire others with your positive attitude and resilience. The future of attitude intelligence is bright, and by continuing your journey, you can create a life filled with success, happiness, and fulfillment.

12.3 Inspiring Others with Attitude Intelligence

Attitude intelligence is not only about personal growth and development; it also has the power to inspire and influence others in a positive way. When we possess a strong attitude intelligence, we become role models and catalysts for change, motivating those around us to adopt a similar mindset. In this section, we will explore how we can inspire others with our attitude intelligence and create a ripple effect of positivity and success.

Leading by Example

One of the most effective ways to inspire others with attitude intelligence is by leading by example. When we consistently demonstrate a positive attitude and approach challenges with resilience and determination, people take notice. Our actions speak louder than words, and when others see us thriving and overcoming obstacles, they are inspired to do the same.

By embodying the principles of attitude intelligence, we become living proof that a positive mindset can lead to success and happiness. Whether it's in our personal relationships, professional life, or any other aspect of life, our attitude becomes a beacon of hope and inspiration for those around us.

Sharing Personal Stories

Another powerful way to inspire others with attitude intelligence is by sharing our personal stories of growth and transformation. When we open up about our own struggles and how we overcame them through a positive attitude, we create a sense of connection and relatability.

By sharing our experiences, we show others that they are not alone in their challenges and that they too can overcome obstacles with the right mindset. Our stories become a source of inspiration and motivation, giving others the courage to face their own difficulties head-on.

Offering Support and Encouragement

Inspiring others with attitude intelligence also involves offering support and encouragement. When we genuinely believe in someone's potential and express our confidence in their abilities, we empower them to believe in themselves. By providing a listening ear, offering guidance, and cheering them on, we become a source of strength and motivation for others.

It's important to remember that inspiring others doesn't mean fixing their problems or taking responsibility for their growth. Instead, it's about creating a supportive environment where they feel empowered to take charge of their own attitude and journey of personal development.

Practicing Empathy and Understanding

Inspiring others with attitude intelligence requires us to practice empathy and understanding. We must recognize that everyone is on their own unique path and may be facing challenges that we cannot fully comprehend. By approaching others with compassion and empathy, we create a safe space for them to open up and share their struggles.

When we listen without judgment and seek to understand their perspective, we can offer guidance and support that is tailored to their needs. By acknowledging their emotions and validating their experiences, we inspire them to adopt a positive attitude and find the strength to overcome their challenges.

Celebrating Successes, Big and Small

Inspiring others with attitude intelligence also involves celebrating their successes, no matter how big or small. By acknowledging and appreciating their achievements, we reinforce the belief that a positive attitude leads to positive outcomes. Whether it's a small step towards a goal or a major accomplishment, every success deserves recognition and celebration.

By celebrating the successes of others, we create a culture of positivity and encouragement. This not only inspires the individual but also motivates others to strive for their own successes. When we highlight the power of attitude in achieving goals, we inspire a collective mindset of growth and resilience.

Being a Source of Positivity

Finally, inspiring others with attitude intelligence means being a source of positivity in their lives. By radiating positivity and optimism, we create an uplifting environment that encourages others to adopt a similar mindset. Our words and actions have the power to influence the attitudes of those around us, so it's important to choose them wisely.

By offering words of encouragement, practicing gratitude, and focusing on solutions rather than problems, we inspire others to see the world through a positive lens. Our attitude becomes contagious, spreading positivity and inspiring others to embrace a similar outlook on life.

In conclusion, attitude intelligence has the power to inspire and influence others in profound ways. By leading by example, sharing personal stories, offering support and encouragement, practicing empathy, celebrating successes, and being a source of positivity, we can inspire those around us to adopt a positive attitude and achieve their own personal growth and success. As we continue our journey of attitude development, let us remember the impact we can have on others and strive to inspire and uplift those around us with our attitude intelligence.

12.4 The Future of Attitude Intelligence

Attitude Intelligence has the potential to revolutionize every aspect of our lives. As we continue to understand the power of attitude and its impact on our well-being, relationships, career, and overall success, the future of Attitude Intelligence holds immense promise.

Embracing Attitude Intelligence in Education

One area where Attitude Intelligence can make a significant difference is in education. As we recognize the importance of a positive attitude in learning, educators are incorporating Attitude Intelligence into their teaching methods. By fostering a growth mindset and emphasizing the value of perseverance and resilience, students are encouraged to approach challenges with a positive attitude. This shift in educational practices can lead to improved academic performance, increased motivation, and a love for lifelong learning.

Attitude Intelligence in the Workplace

The future of Attitude Intelligence in the professional world is also promising. As organizations realize the impact of employee attitudes on productivity, job satisfaction, and overall success, they are investing in programs and initiatives to develop Attitude Intelligence in their workforce. Companies are recognizing that a positive attitude can enhance teamwork, creativity, and problem-solving abilities. By fostering a culture of positivity and providing training in Attitude Intelligence, organizations can create a more harmonious and productive work environment.

Attitude Intelligence and Technology

With the rapid advancement of technology, Attitude Intelligence has the potential to play a significant role in shaping our digital experiences. As artificial intelligence and machine learning become more integrated into our daily lives, the development of emotional intelligence and positive attitudes will become increasingly important.

Attitude Intelligence can help us navigate the complexities of technology, ensuring that we maintain a healthy balance between the virtual and real world. By promoting empathy, mindfulness, and responsible use of technology, we can harness its benefits while safeguarding our mental and emotional well-being.

Attitude Intelligence and Health

The future of Attitude Intelligence in the realm of health and well-being is also promising. Research has shown that a positive attitude can have a profound impact on physical health, mental well-being, and emotional resilience. As we continue to explore the mind-body connection, Attitude Intelligence can be integrated into healthcare practices to promote holistic healing. By incorporating positive psychology, mindfulness techniques, and attitude-focused interventions, healthcare professionals can empower individuals to take an active role in their own well-being.

Attitude Intelligence and Social Change

Attitude Intelligence has the potential to drive positive social change. As individuals develop their Attitude Intelligence, they become more empathetic, compassionate, and culturally sensitive. This heightened awareness and understanding can lead to greater inclusivity, tolerance, and acceptance in society. Attitude Intelligence can inspire individuals to take action, advocate for social justice, and work towards creating a more equitable and harmonious world.

Attitude Intelligence and Personal Growth

The future of Attitude Intelligence lies in its continued integration into personal growth and development. As individuals recognize the power of their attitudes in shaping their lives, they are actively seeking ways to enhance their Attitude Intelligence. This includes engaging in practices such as gratitude journaling, mindfulness meditation, and self-reflection. By cultivating a positive attitude and developing emotional resilience, individuals can overcome challenges, achieve their goals, and lead fulfilling lives.

The Role of Research and Education

To fully realize the potential of Attitude Intelligence, ongoing research and education are crucial. Continued scientific exploration can deepen our understanding of the mechanisms behind Attitude Intelligence and its impact on various aspects of life. This research can inform the development of evidence-based interventions and strategies to enhance Attitude Intelligence in individuals and communities.

Education plays a vital role in spreading awareness and knowledge about Attitude Intelligence. By incorporating Attitude Intelligence into school curricula, workshops, and training programs, we can equip future generations with the tools they need to navigate life's challenges with a positive attitude.

Conclusion

The future of Attitude Intelligence is bright and promising. As we continue to recognize the profound impact of attitude on every aspect of our lives, we can harness its power to create positive change. By embracing Attitude Intelligence in education, the workplace, technology, health, social interactions, and personal growth, we can shape a future where individuals and communities thrive. Through ongoing research, education, and personal development, we can unlock the full potential of Attitude Intelligence and create a world filled with positivity, resilience, and success.

https://x.com/
Phoenixhei22036?t=Y4rgrw3NUf5OFfl4oN4B9A&s=09
https://www.facebook.com/profile.php?id=100090731780769

It is on God and you

MAINTAINING THE RIGHT ATTITUDE IN THE LAST MINUTE

IT IS THE UNVEILING of man's attitudes and temperaments that defines him and positions him when he is faced with situations in life. Life is all about action and reaction. Life's dependency is on our relationship with God Almighty and man.

Don't miss out!

Visit the website below and you can sign up to receive emails whenever BANTAR-SHEY publishes a new book. There's no charge and no obligation.

https://books2read.com/r/B-A-AZEBB-REXPC

BOOKS2READ

Connecting independent readers to independent writers.

About the Author

Bantar-Shey is a young Gospel Minister. He is inspired by the works of God and led by the Holy Spirit, to write this piece of revelation for you. He is a holder of a Master's degree in Marketing, a Bachelor's degree in Technology in Marketing, and a Higher National Diploma (H.N.D.) in Marketing. He also has multiple certifications in Tech, Counseling, and Sports Marketing. He is also a Scriptwriter.

Read more at https://koji.to/@bantarshey3000.

About the Publisher

A conglomerate. We are into book publishing, proofreading, translation, real estate, entertainment, marketing & more
Read more at https://koji.to/@bantarshey3000.